MARIA FINN

MEXICO IN MIND

Maria Finn is the editor of the anthology *Cuba in Mind* (Vintage, 2004) and author of a memoir about falling in love and marrying her cab driver in Havana, Cuba. It will be published in 2007 by Algonquin Books. She has written for *Audubon*, *Saveur*, *Metropolis*, *The New York Times*, and the *Los Angeles Times*, among many other publications. She has an MFA in Creative Writing from Sarah Lawrence College and has published literary work in magazines such as *Gastronomica*, *The Chicago Review*, *New Letters*, and *Exquisite Corpse*. She has lived and worked in Alaska, Guatemala, and Spain, and traveled extensively in Latin America.

Visit her website at www.mariafinndominguez.com.

D0047903

Cuba in Mind, edited by Maria Finn Dominguez

France in Mind, edited by Alice Leccese Powers

India in Mind, edited by Pankaj Mishra

Ireland in Mind, edited by Alice Leccese Powers

Italy in Mind, edited by Alice Leccese Powers

Paris in Mind, edited by Jennifer Lee

Tuscany in Mind, edited by Alice Leccese Powers

MEXICO IN MIND

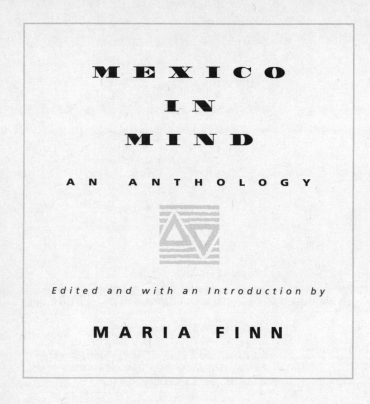

MEXICO IN MIND

AN ANTHOLOGY

Edited and with an Introduction by

MARIA FINN

Vintage Departures

VINTAGE BOOKS

A DIVISION OF RANDOM HOUSE, INC.

NEW YORK

FIRST VINTAGE DEPARTURES EDITION, JUNE 2006

Copyright © 2006 by Maria Finn

All rights reserved. Published in the United States by Vintage Books,
a division of Random House, Inc., New York, and in Canada
by Random House of Canada Limited, Toronto.

Vintage is a registered trademark and Vintage Departures
and colophon are trademarks of Random House, Inc.

Pages 233–35 constitute an extension of the copyright page.

The Cataloging-in-Publication Data is on file at the Library of Congress.

Vintage ISBN-10: 0-307-27488-8
Vintage ISBN-13: 978-0-307-27488-5

Book design by Jo Anne Metsch

www.vintagebooks.com

Printed in the United States of America
10 9 8 7 6 5 4 3 2

CONTENTS

Introduction / *xi*

LOVE IN MEXICO / 1
Bésame Mucho

ALICE ADAMS / *3*
  from *Mexico: Some Travels and Some Travelers There* (1991)

EDWARD WESTON / *9*
  from *The Daybooks of Edward Weston* (1923)

KATHERINE ANNE PORTER / *19*
  "The Martyr" (1923)

MURIEL RUKEYSER / *26*
  "Evening Plaza, San Miguel" (1944)

RAY BRADBURY / *28*
  "Calling Mexico" (1950)

JOHN STEINBECK / *35*
  from *The Pearl* (1945)

LUIS RODRIGUEZ / *42*
  "The Old Woman of Mérida" (2005)

SIGHTS, SOUNDS, AND TASTES / 45
Fiesta del Pueblo

FRANCES CALDERÓN DE LA BARCA / 47
from *Life in Mexico* (1843)

FANNY CHAMBERS GOOCH INGLEHART / 53
from *Face to Face with the Mexicans* (1887)

CHARLES MACOMB FLANDRAU / 57
from *Viva Mexico!* (1908)

D. H. LAWRENCE / 66
from *Mornings in Mexico* (1927)

DIANA KENNEDY / 73
from *My Mexico* (1998)

TOM MILLER / 81
from "Searching for the Heart of La Bamba," in *Jack Ruby's Kitchen Sink* (2000)

REVOLUTIONARY ENCOUNTERS / 87
¡Que Viva Mexico!

ARCHIBALD MACLEISH / 89
from *Conquistador* (1932)

JOHN REED / 92
from *Insurgent Mexico* (1914)

ANITA DESAI / 106
from *The Zigzag Way* (2004)

GRAHAM GREENE / 115
from *Another Mexico* (1939)

ANN LOUISE BARDACH / 121
from "Mexico's Poet Rebel" (1994)

DOWN AND OUT IN MEXICO / *133*
Desperados

TENNESSEE WILLIAMS / *135*
from *Night of the Iguana* (1961)

MALCOLM LOWRY / *149*
from *Under the Volcano* (1947)

JACK KEROUAC / *154*
from "Mexico Fellaheen" (1960)

WILLIAM S. BURROUGHS / *159*
from *Junky* (1953)

DONNA M. GERSHTEN / *167*
from *Kissing the Virgin's Mouth* (2000)

ICONS AND IDENTITY / *171*
Patria and Pilgrims

RICHARD RODRIGUEZ / *173*
from *Days of Obligation* (1992)

ANA CASTILLO / *178*
"My Mother's México" (1994)

RUBÉN MARTÍNEZ / *190*
from *Crossing Over* (2001)

SANDRA CISNEROS / *201*
"You Bring Out the Mexican in Me" (1994)

RITUAL AND MYTH / *205*
Día de los Muertos and Beyond

ERNA FERGUSSON / *207*
from *Fiesta in Mexico* (1934)

LANGSTON HUGHES / *213*
   from *The Big Sea* (1940)

GARY JENNINGS / *216*
   from *Aztec* (1980)

SALMAN RUSHDIE / *224*
   from *The Ground Beneath Her Feet* (1999)

INTRODUCTION

Mexico in Mind offers a sampling of travelers' impressions of Mexico over the span of two centuries. There are many Mexicos here: D. H. Lawrence writes about "the spark of contact" on market day near Oaxaca, Charles Macomb Flandrau describes life on a coffee plantation in Chiapas, the cultural fusions of Veracruz are explored by Tom Miller, the feeling of dusk in a Mexican plaza is evoked by poet Muriel Rukeyser, William Burroughs reveals the lawless underside of Mexico City, Ray Bradbury shows us a dying man's nostalgia for the city's bustle and life.

This anthology has been shaped both by my trips to Mexico and by my extended family, which has given me a more personal connection to the place. I've traveled to several places in Mexico over the course of many years and now my memories of the trips are like snapshots: the cool, dry plaza in Oaxaca, the surrounding mountains blue-hued in evening light; Chiapas, with indigenous people wearing brightly woven *huipiles* and the vinegary scent of drying coffee filling the air; tasting mango sprinkled with chili powder while sitting on the seawall of Veracruz; the turquoise lagoons near Cancún and the view from the tops of Mayan pyramids; the energy and hum of Mexico City, from magnificent museums to plazas filled with mariachi musicians. And the no-man's-land feel of the raw Chihuahuan desert surrounding Ciudad Juárez, just over the border from El Paso, Texas.

My three brothers live in El Paso, and all three of them are married to women from Mexico. When I started this project, my mother protested. "You can't create a *Mexico in Mind*," she said. "It's too much. There needs to be a *Mexico City in Mind*, a *Oaxaca in Mind*. There are more than eleven types of indigenous people in Oaxaca alone." She's right in a way. I found Mexico, fascinating and beautiful as it is, to be an enormous, complex place that I couldn't possibly come to know in one lifetime, let alone convey in one volume.

In Mexico, history is alive. Revolutions inspire future revolutions, and the names of the movements' heroes resurface in different times and places. The names one hears called out of doorways to playing children carry on Mexico's legends. My sister-in-law Nohemi named her first son Emiliano, for the great revolutionary Emiliano Zapata, and her second son Cuauhtémoc for the Aztec king who tried to fend off the Spaniards after Montezuma handed over the empire. I've included an excerpt from Gary Jennings's novel *Aztec* that recreates Cuauhtémoc's time in history, and while trying to select a portion of Anita Desai's lovely novel *The Zigzag Way*, I'm sure I was influenced by my little nephew named for a revolutionary when I decided on a passage where insurgents led by Pancho Villa and Emiliano Zapata disrupt the mining industry.

Journalist John Reed rode with those revolutionaries, even spending time with Pancho Villa himself and chronicling it in his book *Insurgent Mexico*. His account of the scrappy soldiers and their families is at times sad, at times humorous, but always lively. Almost a century later, another intrepid journalist, Ann Louise Bardach, traveled to the Chiapas region to interview Subcomandante Marcos, a legendary leader of the Zapatista Revolution.

Nohemi, my brother, and their children moved into a suburb

with large beige and white houses just over the border of Texas into New Mexico. The woman who lived in the house before Nohemi had been asked by neighbors if she was the cleaning woman. She had been the only Mexican on the block. When Nohemi moved in, she had the house painted bright orange with blue trim to make sure nobody asked her that question. In no subtle way, the colors say "Mexican owner on the block." There are particular shades of blue and orange that can be identified as "Mexican" throughout the world. This is in no small part due to the paintings of Frida Kahlo and murals of Diego Rivera, whose art has made the bold, bright colors popular in Mexico recognizable worldwide. Diego Rivera appears three times in this collection, once in the journals of photographer Edward Weston, who was his friend and contemporary during what is now known as "The Mexican Renaissance," and also in a short story by Katherine Anne Porter, where she fictionalizes his relationship with the beauty Lupe Marin. Alice Adams uses a visit to Frida Kahlo's house to write about Kahlo's art and her tempestuous relationship with Rivera.

Another sister-in-law of mine, Raquel, left central Mexico with her mother and seven siblings when her father died. Despite the difficulty of growing up as an immigrant in Los Angeles, or perhaps in part due to it, she is a gentle, considerate person who over the years has patiently taught me many things, including how to cook a few Mexican dishes. During Christmas at her house we have *sopes* made of masa dough and a warm drink, *calientitos* of stewed fruit and sugarcane. Anytime she sees a jar of store-bought salsa, I see her struggling not to make a face and politely pretending she didn't see it. She's taught me to make tomatillo salsa and chipotle sauce, among other marvels. Mexican food is sensuous and creative, whether street food bought from a vendor—grilled corn rubbed with lime and sprinkled with chili powder—or a restaurant's *chiles enogadas*, peppers stuffed with pomegranates and almond paste. I have become a big fan of Diana Kennedy, known as "the high priestess of Mexican cooking," and her books on Mexican cuisine. Her excerpt here gives a glimpse of the ritual and creativity of regional Mexican cooking.

Raquel's son, Casito, as a toddler thought anything bright and hanging was a piñata. That and his fierce sweet tooth led him one holiday season to beat the Christmas stockings right off their hooks. My brother Casey insists that piñatas are one of Mexico's great cultural exports, and he suggested that I include them in the anthology. The description that I found of breaking the piñata written by Fanny Gooch Inglehart in 1887 is a scene that could just as easily have taken place today.

My third sister-in-law Hilda's two children, Priscilla and Andrew, switch back and forth between the English language and Spanish seamlessly. They go to school in El Paso, but take art and dance lessons in Juárez. They speak Spanish to one set of grandparents and English to the other. When I look at my little niece and nephews, it is apparent that in many ways our countries are fusing. What was once the "other" is becoming much more familiar for both sides. The essay "My Mother's México," by Ana Castillo, looks at the influences at play between countries as she moves back and forth on family visits. Mexican-American Richard Rodriguez explains the lure of the revered Virgin of Guadalupe for Mexicans on both sides of the border and the puzzle of nationality and identity.

When my parents visit El Paso, all three daughters-in-law argue over hosting them, and then treat them like royalty when they are in their homes. Through my sisters-in-law, I've come to learn not only about hardship in Mexico and discrimination against Mexicans in the United States, but also about the warmth, generosity, humor, and spirit of Mexico.

Each of my visits to Mexico has been unsatisfying to me in the sense that I just want to go back and see more. I hope the literary journey in *Mexico in Mind* has a similar effect, inspiring readers to follow what interests them most and seek out and read the sources in their entirety. From reading all of Gary Jennings's novel *Aztec*, I know the identity of the "filth goddess" mentioned in Sandra Cisneros's poem "You Bring Out the Mexican in Me." When reading *Crossing Over*, Rubén Martínez's tale of a tragic border crossing, a quote that I'd come across in Graham Greene's *Another Mexico* reverberated within me: "The atmosphere of the border—it is like starting over again; there is something about it like a good confession: poised for a few happy moments between sin and sin. When people die on the border, they call it 'a happy death.'" I've tried to link the excerpts as best I can, but there are limits to what fits between two covers. This is what is wonderful about an anthology, unlike other types of books—it never really ends. Just like traveling in Mexico.

MEXICO IN MIND

LOVE
IN MEXICO

Bésame Mucho

ALICE ADAMS

(1926–99)

Alice Adams is the author of ten novels and five collections of short stories, including *Careless Love* (1966), *Superior Women* (1984), *Caroline's Daughters* (1991), *Almost Perfect* (1993), *A Southern Exposure* (1995), and its sequel, the posthumously published *After the War* (2000). She's known for looking at the lives of contemporary women, exploring the nuances of both their professional and personal worlds and the intersection of the two.

Adams traveled annually to Mexico for approximately thirty years. In this excerpt from *Mexico: Some Travels and Some Travelers There* (1991), she is inspired by an exhibit of Frida Kahlo's art in San Francisco to visit the artist's home, now a museum. Kahlo's art reflects both her love for Mexico and her often painful love for fellow artist Diego Rivera. She has become an icon for the suffering artist. According to Adams, "Two words often used in connection with Kahlo are narcissism ('All those self-portraits') and masochism ('All that blood'). Both seem to me quite wrongly applied. I rather believe Kahlo painted herself and her images of personal pain in an effort to stave off madness and death."

When I thought of a return trip to Mexico City, with some friends who had never been there before, I remembered the Camino Real, which would be as far out of the fumes and the general turmoil as one could get, I thought—with advertisements featuring three swimming pools.

And this trip's true object, twenty years after my first contact with her, was Frida Kahlo: I wanted to make a pilgrimage to her house, and I had talked two friends into coming with me—Gloria, a writer, and Mary, an art critic.

All of this more or less began in the spring of eighty-seven, when there was an extraordinary exhibit of Kahlo's work at the Galería de la Raza, in San Francisco. So many painters' work is weakened by its mass presentation in a show, but this was not so with Kahlo's work: The overall effect was cumulative, brilliantly power-ful, almost overwhelming. Her sheer painterly skill is often over-looked in violent reactions, one way or another, to her subject matter, but only consummate skill could have produced such meticulous images of pain, and love, and loneliness.

I began to sense then, in San Francisco, a sort of ground swell of interest in both her work and in her life—and the two are inex-tricable. Kahlo painted what she felt as the central facts of her life: her badly maimed but still beautiful body, and her violent love for Diego. In fact, these days Frida has become a heroine of several groups; she is a heroine as an artist; as a Third World woman; and also as a handicapped woman. And then there is still another group popularly referred to as "women who love too much," the "too much" referring especially to men perceived as bad, as unfaithful and not loving enough in return.

I began to read all I could about Frida Kahlo.

The accident that maimed her occurred when she was eighteen: A streetcar rammed into the trolley in which she was riding, and her spine was broken in seventeen places—it is astonishing that she should have survived. Her pelvis was penetrated by a shaft of metal (a "rape" of which Frida made much), her reproductive organs were gravely injured.

Considerable controversy continues over the precise facts about her injuries. Medical records are lost, or missing. It is now impossible to determine whether she actually did, as she claimed, have seventeen corrective operations; Frida did tend to exaggerate, to mythologize herself, but even a dozen such operations would be quite a lot. It is also uncertain whether she could or could not bear children, or whether she really wanted to. Certainly she was pregnant a number of times and suffered both therapeutic abortions and miscarriages. It would seem to me that she was extremely ambivalent, to say the least, about having children.

She was not ambivalent about Diego; she adored him, she loved him too much.

In the course, then, of reading about Frida, of looking at what paintings I could (even in reproduction they are, to me, both intensely beautiful and powerfully moving), and of talking to a few Kahlo scholars, one of the first things that I learned about her was that, in addition to her extraordinary and absolutely original talent, Frida had a capacity for inspiring feelings of an exceptional intensity in almost anyone who encountered her. And she would seem to continue to do so, even in death. (I should here admit my own enthrallment, with which I seem to have infected my friends, Gloria and Mary.) Thus, a trip to the Frida Kahlo Museum, which was formerly her home, the blue house out in Coyoacán, is apt to have the character of a pilgrimage to a shrine. We went there to pay homage as well as out of curiosity. And we had, I am sure, like all passionate pilgrims, a burden of expectations, or preconceptions, some quite possibly unconscious.

In any case, the museum contained some vast surprises: considerable beauty, much sadness, and several disturbing questions.

The first surprise for me was quite simply the intensity of the color of those high outer walls; to a Californian (I suppose I am one), the phrase "blue house" implies a pastel, surely not the violent, vibrant blue of Frida's house, which is like certain Mexican skies. Its size, too, was unexpected: It covers a small town block.

High walls, then, and a gate guarded by two papier-mâché judas figures—and by a small, somewhat shabby real guard, who assures visitors that their entrance is free and warns them that they may not take pictures.

To the right, just as one passes between the judas giants, there is a small room with a glassed-in counter and some shelves, obviously designed as a bookstore postcard display area—and now quite bare. Empty, that is, except for one rather gaudy pamphlet, entitled "Altar in the First Centenary of Diego Rivera," and in which there are many references to, and an introduction by, Dolores Olmeda, the "Life Director of the Diego Rivera and Frida Kahlo Museums." Frida is mentioned only once, as Diego's third wife. No books on Frida, no posters or postcards. (*Why?*)

The garden area that one next sees is rich and wonderful, however: a barely tamed green jungle, a perfect habitat for Frida's pet monkeys, for birds. (Cats would love it there, I thought, not seeing any.) At the time of my visit a large bed of pink lilies blossomed, the kind called Naked Ladies. And great tall trees. And a tangled profusion of vines.

On a wall near the entrance to Frida's house an inscription informed us that Frida and Diego had lived in this house from 1929 to 1954—a touching announcement and quite untrue (and who put it there, I wonder?). For although Frida was born in that house, which was built by her father, Diego's residences were both multiple and brief; he came and went very much as he chose, neither remaining at home nor staying away for long (one knows the type). The abode most lengthily shared by Frida and Diego is the two joined houses in San Angel, now the Diego Rivera Museum.

The first room of the blue house is rather low and small, as are all the rooms in this semicolonial sprawl. One can imagine the house as warm and wonderful, hospitable first to the large Kahlo group (her father by two wives had six daughters), and then to Frida and Diego and their enormous circle of friends: Trotsky,

Siqueiros, et cetera. But it takes considerable imagining, so little household furniture is left (and whatever happened to it? Where are all the ordinary tables and chairs that were used by Frida?).

Frida's paintings line this entrance room, and while interesting and highly original, as is all her work, they are simply not her best; in no sense is this a major Kahlo exhibition—a great pity, since her work is extremely hard to find. Most of her paintings are in private collections, including all the paintings that she willed to Rivera and that he in turn willed to a trust for the people of Mexico, along with her house. She is barely represented in museums in Mexico City.

The most striking of that small collection is the bright still life of watermelons, *Viva la Vida*, thus titled and signed by Frida very shortly before her death. But this painting's appeal seems emotional and historic, rather than intrinsic.

The kitchen is cozily furnished indeed, with bright painted chairs, red and yellow, new-looking (too new to have been there when Frida was), the sort that one might find in any Mexican open market. And glazed plates and pottery, cooking implements. Tiny jars affixed to the back wall, high up, spell out *Frida y Diego* in large letters. This seemed an unlikely note of kitsch, and indeed I was later told that these names were a later addition, put up some years after the deaths of Diego and Frida.

Other rooms house an extensive collection of pre-Columbian figures, and paintings, mostly by Rivera, some by friends, both Mexican and European. And there is Diego's bedroom, with his surprisingly small bed for such a huge man, and his rough, enormous boots. Then, going upstairs, within the broad, dark stairwell is the vast collection of *retablos*, small Mexican votive paintings, said to have profoundly influenced the art of Frida.

And then one comes to Frida's tiny, narrow, poignant bedroom, the room in which, at forty-seven, she died and was laid out. And photographed, lying there.

Since she was so very, very often photographed in life (more often than Marilyn Monroe, it has been said)—the daughter of a photographer, she must have been early habituated to what seems to many people an intrusion—it is not surprising that she was also photographed in death, on this same narrow white bed, with its florally embroidered sheets. One of the terrible plaster casts that she finally had to wear (and that she decorated with painted flowers) lies on the coverlet. Still, this sense of her death makes visiting this area both macabre and embarrassing: I felt that I should not have been there.

It seems more permissible to enter the studio, built for her by Diego, in 1946, and wonderfully open to views of her wild green garden. It is a cheering, open room, and one can forgive Diego a great deal for having built this space for Frida's work.

Which leads us to a question that often seems to trouble Frida's partisans: Why did Frida remain in such a state of adoration for a man who was continuously, compulsively unfaithful to her, and who was for long periods of time conspicuously off and away with other, often famous, women? It seems to me that there are two explanations, insofar as one can "explain" a major passion—one rational, one not. The rational explanation would be that Diego entirely supported Frida's work; he often spoke of her as one of the greatest living painters, he cited the intensely female, anguished complexity of her work. He even compared his own painting unfavorably to hers (quite correctly, in my own view).

And, more darkly, irrationally, Frida was absolutely addicted to Diego; she could be said to have been impaled on her mania for Diego, as she had been literally impaled in the horrifying streetcar accident that, when she was eighteen, so painfully, horribly transformed her life. She herself referred to the "two accidents" in her life, the streetcar crash and Diego.

EDWARD WESTON

(1 8 8 6 – 1 9 5 8)

Born in Highland Park, Illinois, Edward Weston first started taking photographs in 1902. He moved to California, where he married and fathered four sons. Weston met Tina Modotti in California about 1919 when he became her mentor and then, two years later, her lover. She modeled for him and helped set up photography connections for him in Mexico City. In 1923, they traveled to Mexico with his eldest son, Chandler; there they became part of what is now known as the Mexican Renaissance, which included artists such as Diego Rivera and José Clemente Orozco. Mexico was just coming out of the revolution, started years earlier by Villa and Zapata, and the atmosphere was politically charged. Modotti became politically involved, and many of her later photographs depict Mexican workers and revolutionary icons. In Mexico, Weston developed a modernist aesthetic and created sharp, clear photographs, frequently sensual depictions of flora and of nudes. Through their work during this time, Weston and Modotti influenced photographers in both Mexico and the United States; they became internationally known for influencing modernist photography as well as for their stormy romance.

The Daybooks are journals kept by Weston, beginning with entries from 1923. They chronicle the three years he spent in Mexico, including observations about places and people, doubts and eagerness about his own work, his financial concerns, and his friendship with Diego Rivera and Lupe Marin, Rivera's beautiful, spirited wife at the time. The journals are an intimate account of his thoughts on Mexico, art, love affairs, and his development as a photographer.

"ROMANTIC MEXICO"

August 2, 1923. Tina, Chandler and Edward on board the S. S. Colima, *four days out from Los Angeles.* At last we are Mexico bound, after months of preparation, after such endless delays that the proposed adventure seemed but a conceit of the imagination never actually to materialize. Each postponement became a joke to our friends and a source of mortification to us. But money had to be raised, and with rumors of my departure many last moment sittings came in, each one helping to secure our future.

Nor was it easy to uproot oneself and part with friends and family—there were farewells which hurt like knife thrusts.

But I adapt myself to change—already Los Angeles seems part of a distant past. The uneventful days—the balmy air has relaxed me—my overstrained nerves are eased. I begin to feel the actuality of this voyage.

The *Colima* flies a Mexican flag, she is small, not too clean and slow—yet I would not change to a more pretentious ship, noisy with passengers from whom there might be no escape. The crew, all Mexican, is colorful and inefficient according to our standards—but it is a relief to escape from that efficiency which makes for mechanized movements, unrelieved drabness.

On board is an Australian sea-captain, a coarse, loud fellow, who continually bellyaches over the dirt, food, service—he goes purple when a waiter's coat is unbuttoned, discounts the whole crew as ignorant, beneath contempt—yet he is the one who suffers by comparison. The Mexicans, at least, have an innate fineness, and they are good to look upon.

Yesterday the sea was rough, the *Colima* pitched and rolled— Tina sick, pobrecita! In contrast, the night before, our ship cut through silent, glassy waters domed by stars—toward what unknown horizons? A night of suspended action—of delayed but imminent climaxes—anything might happen—nothing did.

August 4. A half-moon half hidden by heavy clouds—sculptured rocks, black, rising from silvered waters—shriek of whistle and rasp of chain; 1:00 A.M. and we anchored in the harbor of Mazatlán, my first foreign port.

Morning—and we excitedly prepared for shore. Thanks to Tina—her beauty—though I might have wished it otherwise!—el Capitán has favored us in many ways: the use of his deck, refreshing drinks in his cabin, his launch to carry us ashore.

Did I visualize what I was to see in my first Mexican port? This is hard to say today—seeing, with stranger's eyes, a stage set: blocks of low houses—a continuous wall of alternate pastel blues, pinks, greens. Down narrow streets Indian boys drove heavy-laden burros; around corners appeared vendors of water or chickens—a half-dozen hanging head down, their legs crossed over a pole, all peeping dolorously.

Street stands sold tropical fruits—some new to me and delicious—for instance, the mango is truly nectar. Aguacates—avocados—sold for 5 centavos! There were vehicles for hire, two-wheeled carts and low-swung coaches. In one of these, drawn by a span of horses—decrepit ones I must admit—we drove along the coast at sunset.

Later, exploring the city streets at night, we found life both gay and sad—sharp clashes of contrasting extremes, but always life—vital, intense, black and white, never grey. Glendale, on the contrary, is drab, spiritless, a uniform grey—peopled by exploiters who have raped a fair land.

Often the barred windows framed lovely black-gowned señoritas—and some not so lovely.

Leisurely drinking ice-cold beer in the patio of Hotel Belmar was a fitting prologue to our first day in Mexico. Later we were introduced to Mexican hospitality when we met the captain at noon "for a cocktail." The party grew from four to a dozen—the drinks progressed from cocktails to tequila straight— Strange how one can understand a foreign tongue with tequila in one's belly.

August 6. Sailing again after two days in Mazatlán.

We did not go ashore again—too hot! Water has poured from my body in rivulets—never before have I perspired so profusely—nor so dishonestly loafed dreamy hours away (this thought reveals my New England background!).

I was tempted in Mazatlán to "go tourist" with my camera, making "snaps" of street scenes—even doing Tina in her grand coach backed by a ruin.

But yesterday I made the first negatives other than matter-of-fact records—negatives with intention. A quite marvellous cloud form tempted me—a sunlit cloud which rose from the bay to become a towering white column.

Mazatlán becomes more vivid in retrospect: I recall cool patios glimpsed from sun-baked streets which sheltered coconut palms, strange lilies, banana trees. I see the cathedral, with its crude Christ, horribly real—and the dramatic devotion of those who come to pray, some sprawled in abject penitence at the entrance before raising their eyes to the glories within.

In the cool twilight hour children danced in the streets—as our carriage approached, they stopped to see the extranjeros—foreigners.

August 8. Three days since leaving the boat. Before dawn we had anchored in the harbor of Manzanillo—by eleven, we had passed the customhouse officials, though not without much palavering, suspicious glances at my battery of lenses, chemicals and personal effects, which Ramiel [McGhee, a close friend] had packed so well that I despaired of ever getting the trunks repacked before train departure.

But there was time to spare, so we wandered the streets escorted by el Capitán, ever attentive. As we sat with our beer looking out to the bluest of seas, a sailor from the *Colima* passed, hesitated, returned; saluting his captain he requested permission to order us drinks. A wandering trio of musicians passed—were hailed by "our" captain—played *Borrachita*—slightly tipsy. My Anglo-Saxon reserve was put to test—and lost. But it was more than the music—the hospitality—the blue sea—which broke my resistance: I knew that this day marked an end—and a beginning.

August 20. Avenida del Hipódromo 3, Colonia Nápoles, Tacubaya, México, D. F.—about 40 minutes by trolley from the city. We have leased an old and beautiful hacienda for six months; ten rooms, each opening onto a spacious patio, 85 × 100 ft., filled with vines, shrubs, trees. The house is of brick with high ceilings and tall arched windows, barred, heavily shuttered, seeming to suggest possible attack. The first night there further stimulated the imagination; I was awakened by gunfire under my very windows—then silence, not even inaudible foot-steps. Well, I did not come here for the ordered calm of a Glendale.

The brick walls of our casa are fifteen inches thick, and plastered in and out. The last occupant had papered the rooms with hideous results, and I, curses be, have been laboriously removing it, while the landlord stands by aghast.

Evidently the middle-class Mexican has no better taste than the middle-class American; the store-windows bear me out with a conglomeration of the most tawdry rubbish imaginable. When the Mexican apes the American he acquires his worst side; and, of course the reverse is true, recalling Mexican or "Spanish" type homes in California. Here, the new architecture is "Hollywood" burlesqued, incongruous beside the beauty of passing culture.

But the past still dominates; old churches stand like impregnable fortresses—quite apart from the new and superficial life which surrounds them. La Catedral is majestic, impressive when its great bells are tolled. "El Zócalo," the square in front, is out of keeping with its bad contemporary sculpture. Nearby two urchins played around a fountain graced by a vapid Venus; impulsively one turned, embraced her, kissed her stony lips, and laughed mischievously.

Beautiful women seem rare—maybe they do not walk the streets—and those of the upper-class dress in execrable taste. Maybe I expected shawls and mantillas! Of course, I except the Indian in native costume, both men and women. Often, they are very beautiful, have poise and dignity. Dregs of humanity are on all sides; maimed, diseased beggars pleading insistently.

The pulquerías—bars—in which the Indian finds solace for his lost glory are the most colorful notes of contemporary life in the city, and the following titles evidence the Indian's romance and imagination.

"Sin Estudio"	Without Thought
"La Primavera"	The Springtime
"Un Viejo Amor"	An Old Love
"El Gato Negro"	The Black Cat
"Las Flores"	The Flowers
"La Camelia"	The Camelia
"La Dama Blanca"	The White Lady
"La Esperanza en el Desierto"	Hope in the Wilderness
"Sobre las Olas"	On the Waves
"La Perla de la Piedad"	The Pearl of Piety
"El Asalto"	The Assault
"La Muerte y la Resurrección"	Death and Resurrection

"Las Primorosas"   The Beautiful Girls
"La Gloria de Juan Silveti" (Juan Silveti being one of the
           popular toreros)

Imagine American saloons with such names! Perhaps, if they had had them, we should never have voted the 18th Amendment. That the Indian also has a sense of humor, I concluded from the following inscription noted on a mulepower truck— "Viva el Rápido"—Hail to the Swift One!

December 9, 1923. Last eve was Diego Rivera's birthday. We were invited to six o'clock chocolate. Rivera arrived late from his work of painting frescoes. He was beaming and of ample proportions. I took him one of my prints for a birthday gift, and he gave me a drawing made for one of his murals in return. I had my choice from his portfolio of sketches, but found it almost impossible to choose. Seldom, if ever, have I so thoroughly enjoyed a portfolio. Diego is a master.

Lupe was stunning as usual. She has much of the Indian, so much a child, never a hypocrite: everything she feels is immediately acted out and we were witness to a burst of emotion unpremeditated and unlooked for. Diego had invited Tina and me to see his drawings, so we escaped from the party, dull, as most parties are, to a side room. Soon Lupe appeared, choking, sneering, raging, head tossing, eyes streaming. "Ha! I invited her to see how you two would act together. I did not want her here—you don't think I wanted her!"—and so on, and on about some woman supposed to have been Diego's love. "Estás loca—completamente loca—You are crazy—completely crazy," was Diego's placid, unruffled defence. Lupe left, still storming, only to return, and this time denounce us for having deserted the party, broken it up, cornering Diego. She was right, but Diego's drawings were more important than the party! We felt uncomfortable—worse, guilty, so prepared to leave. Penitent, Lupe came to Tina with a present—two gourds, fantastically painted, a peace offering. I am to photograph her soon.

Today the first order from a sitting in Mexico, 3 prints—110 pesos. No platinum paper yet—ordered a month ago from England.

November 19, Evening. Diego and Lupe Rivera were just in, this time cooing like turtle-doves. It was "niño" this and "niña" that, and she wore a new coral necklace. "In Guadalajara, they thought Diego was my father," laughed Lupe, "and when I told them he was my husband, they said, 'How could you marry such an elephant?'"

Diego looked at my Picasso etching—"I saw Picasso etch that, it was done in December 1908—I don't know why he dated it 1905—at a time when he was in his cubist period. Many said he had forgotten how to draw, so he did that, among others, to disprove them. Picasso had a failing, he was always falling in love with the sweethearts of his friends—hence, continually in trouble."

I showed Rivera some of Chandler's stencil designs and he seemed greatly interested. Chandler has done some very fine things, and out of a clear sky—at least, I can't figure where the influence, if any. Chandler's photographs have been interesting too—one I would have been happy to have made myself. I can see my influence in these, yet they were made entirely unaided. Chandler has had to shift for himself, and having no playmates for baseball or marbles has amused himself by creating.

El Convento de Churubusco is a gem. I think it is the loveliest of the churches I have yet seen, though they should hardly be compared—each having its own special charm. Churubusco is intimate, I wanted to linger and rest in its tiny patio, to caress its mellow tiles, to worship before its lovely golden virgin.

The rest of the party made photographs, one man being a wealthy amateur. I did not, for the churches in Mexico are an end in themselves, needing no further interpretation. I stand before them mute—nothing that I might record could add to their beauty.

Previous to visiting Churubusco, we went to el Convento de la Merced. We met Dr. Atl, who lives there. "I should like to photograph you here, Doctor." "All right." Dr. Atl's "all right" is part of him. His real name is Gerardo Murillo, "Atl" being Indian for water; and "Nahui Olin" is also Indian, standing for the "four movements of the sun." Nahui's real name is Carmen Mondragón. Nahui's books may be interesting, but written in French and Spanish I can make no comment. But neither her paintings nor Atl's have great value, indeed some of his murals I thought very bad, full of half-baked metaphysical striving. But Diego Rivera is so outstanding a figure in Mexican art that much of the rest seem trifling by comparison.

A tiny chapel stands in the centre of a busy market place on Callejón de Manzanares, near the convent. It is quite unpretentious, no carved facade, nor blue and yellow tiles, only bare walls of pastel pink and swirling streams of Indians flowing around it.

November 21. The second order in, this time from Americans here from Tampico, it amounted to 280 pesos, 8 prints from six negatives, a task ahead—six enlarged negatives! So far I have made all my sittings with the Graflex out-of-doors. We eat for another month!

At Churubusco, I picked a daisy to send to Margarethe.

November 24. A few more names noted on the pulquerías:

Charros no Fifis	Cowboys not Dandies
Los Hombres Sabios sin Estudio	Men Wise without Study

La Hermosa Ester	The Beautiful Esther
Mis Illusiones	My Illusions
Las Fieras	The Fierce Ones
El Gallo de Oro	The Cock of Gold
Alegria del Amor	The Ecstacy of Love

Llewellyn left this morning. I watched the train pull out with much sadness. He has been a delightful and lovable friend. Though his piano, at times, was sorely distracting and his dog a damned nuisance.

KATHERINE ANNE PORTER

(1 8 9 0 – 1 9 8 0)

Katherine Anne Porter is best known for her only full-length novel, *Ship of Fools*, which she spent twenty years writing. Upon its publication in 1962, it became a best seller and was made into a major film in 1965. That same year, Porter's *Collected Short Stories* won the National Book Award and the Pulitzer Prize for fiction.

Katherine Anne Porter was born in Indian Creek, Texas, and left at an early age, for marriage and to pursue an acting career. After contracting tuberculosis, she turned to journalism to support herself, working in Chicago and Denver before leaving for Mexico around 1920. There, she was intrigued by the revolutionary politics of the time. She worked as a journalist and a teacher in Mexico, and became acquainted with the leaders of the revolutionary government, including President Álvaro Obregón, and the muralists, including Diego Rivera. Mexico inspired some of her early short stories, including this one, "The Martyr" (1923), which satirizes the relationship between Diego Rivera and Lupe Marín.

THE MARTYR

Rubén, the most illustrious painter in Mexico, was deeply in love with his model Isabel, who was in turn romantically attached to a rival artist whose name is of no importance.

Isabel used to call Rubén her little "Churro," which is a sort of sweet cake, and is, besides, a popular pet name among the Mexicans for small dogs. Rubén thought it a very delightful name, and would say before visitors to the studio, "And now she calls me 'Churro!' Ha! ha!" When he laughed, he shook in the waistcoat, for he was getting fat.

Then Isabel, who was tall and thin, with long, keen fingers, would rip her hands through a bouquet of flowers Rubén had brought her and scatter the petals, or she would cry, "Yah! yah!" derisively, and flick the tip of his nose with paint. She had been observed also to pull his hair and ears without mercy.

When earnest-minded people made pilgrimages down the narrow, cobbled street, picked their way carefully over puddles in the patio, and clattered up the uncertain stairs for a glimpse of the great and yet so simple personage, she would cry, "Here come the pretty sheep!" She enjoyed their gaze of wonder at her daring.

Often she was bored, for sometimes she would stand all day long, braiding and unbraiding her hair while Rubén made sketches of her, and they would forget to eat until late; but there was no place for her to go until her lover, Rubén's rival, should sell a painting, for everyone declared Rubén would kill on sight the man who even attempted to rob him of Isabel. So Isabel stayed, and Rubén made eighteen different drawings of her for his mural, and she cooked for him occasionally, quarreled with him, and put out her long, red tongue at visitors she did not like. Rubén adored her.

He was just beginning the nineteenth drawing of Isabel when his rival sold a very large painting to a rich man whose decorator told him he must have a panel of green and orange on a certain wall of his new house. By a felicitous chance, this painting was prodigiously green and orange. The rich man paid him a huge price, but was happy to do it, he explained, because it would cost six times as much to cover the space with tapestry. The rival was happy, too, though he neglected to explain why. The next day he and Isabel went to Costa Rica, and that is the end of them so far as we are concerned.

Rubén read her farewell note:

Poor old Churro! It is a pity your life is so very dull, and I cannot live it any longer. I am going away with someone who will never allow me to cook for him, but will make a mural with fifty figures of me in it, instead of only twenty. I am also to have red slippers, and a gay life to my heart's content.

Your old friend,
ISABEL

When Rubén read this, he felt like a man drowning. His breath would not come, and he thrashed his arms about a great deal. Then he drank a large bottle of *tequila*, without lemon or salt to take the edge off, and lay down on the floor with his head in a palette of freshly mixed paint and wept vehemently.

After this, he was altogether a changed man. He could not talk unless he was telling about Isabel, her angelic face, her pretty little tricks and ways: "She used to kick my shins black and blue," he would say, fondly, and the tears would flow into his eyes. He was always eating crisp sweet cakes from a bag near his easel. "See," he would say, holding one up before taking a mouthful, "she used to call me 'Churro,' like this!"

His friends were all pleased to see Isabel go, and said among themselves he was lucky to lose the lean she-devil. They set themselves to help him forget. But Rubén could not be distracted. "There is no other woman like that woman," he would say, shaking his head stubbornly. "When she went, she took my life with her. I have no spirit even for revenge." Then he would add, "I tell you, my poor little angel Isabel is a murderess, for she has broken my heart."

At times he would roam anxiously about the studio, kicking his felt slippers into the shuffles of drawings piled about, gathering dust, or he would grind colors for a few minutes, saying in a dolorous voice: "She once did all this for me. Imagine her goodness!" But always he came back to the window, and ate sweets and fruits

and almond cakes from the bag. When his friends took him out
for dinner, he would sit quietly and eat huge platefuls of every sort
of food, and wash it down with sweet wine. Then he would begin
to weep, and talk about Isabel.

His friends agreed it was getting rather stupid. Isabel had been
gone for nearly six months, and Rubén refused even to touch the
nineteenth figure of her, much less to begin the twentieth, and the
mural was getting nowhere.

"Look, my dear friend," said Ramón, who did caricatures, and
heads of pretty girls for the magazines, "even I, who am not a
great artist, know how women can spoil a man's work for him. Let
me tell you, when Trinidad left me, I was good for nothing for a
week. Nothing tasted properly, I could not tell one color from
another, I positively was tone deaf. That shameless cheat-by-night
almost ruined me. But you, *amigo*, rouse yourself, and finish your
great mural for the world, for the future, and remember Isabel
only when you give thanks to God that she is gone."

Rubén would shake his head as he sat collapsed upon his couch
munching sugared almonds, and would cry:

"I have a pain in my heart that will kill me. There is no woman
like that one."

His collars suddenly refused to meet under his chin. He loos-
ened his belt three notches, and explained: "I sit still; I cannot
move any more. My energy has gone to grief." The layers of fat
piled insidiously upon him, he bulged until he became strange
even to himself. Ramón, showing his new caricature of Rubén to
his friends, declared: "I could as well have drawn it with a compass, I swear. The buttons are bursting from his shirt. It is positively unsafe."

But still Rubén sat, eating moodily in solitude, and weeping
over Isabel after his third bottle of sweet wine at night.

His friends talked it over, concluded that the affair was growing
desperate; it was high time someone should tell him the true cause

of his pain. But everyone wished the other would be the one cho-sen. And it came out there was not a person in the group, possibly not one in all Mexico, indelicate enough to do such a thing. They decided to shift the responsibility upon a physician from the fac-ulty of the university. In the mind of such a one would be com-bined a sufficiently refined sentiment with the highest degree of technical knowledge. This was the diplomatic, the discreet, the fastidious thing to do. It was done.

The doctor found Rubén seated before his easel, facing the half-finished nineteenth figure of Isabel. He was weeping, and between sobs he ate spoonfuls of soft Toluca cheese, with spiced mangos. He hung in all directions over his painting-stool, like a mound of kneaded dough. He told the doctor first about Isabel. "I do assure you faithfully, my friend, not even I could capture in paint the line of beauty in her thigh and instep. And, besides, she was an angel for kindness." Later he said the pain in his heart would be the death of him. The doctor was profoundly touched. For a great while he sat offering consolation without courage to prescribe material cures for a man of such delicately adjusted sus-ceptibilities.

"I have only crass and vulgar remedies"—with a graceful ges-ture he seemed to offer them between thumb and forefinger—"but they are all the world of flesh may contribute toward the healing of the wounded spirit." He named them one at a time. They made a neat, but not impressive, row: a diet, fresh air, long walks, frequent violent exercise, preferably on the cross-bar, ice showers, almost no wine.

Rubén seemed not to hear him. His sustained, oblivious mur-mur flowed warmly through the doctor's solemnly rounded pe-riods:

"The pains are most unendurable at night, when I lie in my lonely bed and gaze at the empty heavens through my narrow win-dow, and I think to myself, 'Soon my grave shall be narrower than that window, and darker than that firmament,' and my heart gives a writhe. Ah, Isabelita, my executioner!'"

The doctor tiptoed out respectfully, and left him sitting there eating cheese and gazing with wet eyes at the nineteenth figure of Isabel.

The friends grew hopelessly bored and left him more and more alone. No one saw him for some weeks except the proprietor of a small café called "The Little Monkeys" where Rubén was accustomed to dine with Isabel and where he now went alone for food.

Here one night quite suddenly Rubén clasped his heart with violence, rose from his chair, and upset the dish of tamales and pepper gravy he had been eating. The proprietor ran to him. Rubén said something in a hurried whisper, made rather an impressive gesture over his head with one arm, and, to say it as gently as possible, died.

His friends hastened the next day to see the proprietor, who gave them a solidly dramatic version of the lamentable episode. Ramón was even then gathering material for an intimate biography of his country's most eminent painter, to be illustrated with large numbers of his own character portraits. Already the dedication was composed to his "Friend and Master, Inspired and Incomparable Genius of Art on the American Continent."

"But what did he say to you," insisted Ramón, "at the final stupendous moment? It is most important. The last words of a great artist, they should be very eloquent. Repeat them precisely, my dear fellow! It will add splendor to the biography, nay, to the very history of art itself, if they are eloquent."

The proprietor nodded his head with the air of a man who understands everything.

"I know, I know. Well, maybe you will not believe me when I tell you that his very last words were a truly sublime message to you, his good and faithful friends, and to the world. He said, gentlemen: 'Tell them I am a martyr to love. I perish in a cause worthy the sacrifice. I die of a broken heart!' and then he said, 'Isabelita, my executioner!' That was all, gentlemen," ended the proprietor, simply and reverently. He bowed his head. They all bowed their heads.

"That was truly magnificent," said Ramón, after the correct interval of silent mourning. "I thank you. It is a superb epitaph. I am most gratified."

"He was also supremely fond of my tamales and pepper gravy," added the proprietor in a modest tone. "They were his final indulgence."

"That shall be mentioned in its place, never fear, my good friend," cried Ramón, his voice crumbling with generous emotion, "with the name of your café, even. It shall be a shrine for artists when this story is known. Trust me faithfully to preserve for the future every smallest detail in the life and the character of this great genius. Each episode has its own sacred, its precious and peculiar interest. Yes, truly, I shall mention the tamales."

MURIEL RUKEYSER

(1913–80)

Muriel Rukeyser published her first collection of poems, *Theory of Flight* (1935), when she was twenty-one and in all penned fifteen books of poetry, two biographies, and one novel, *The Orgy*. Muriel Rukeyser's life and work were deeply influenced by her involvement in political issues, from civil rights in the United States to the Spanish Civil War, and later, the United States' involvement in Vietnam. She served as president of PEN American Center to fight for the human rights of writers around the world. Her poetry has won numerous awards, including the National Book Award and the National Book Critics Circle Award, as well as the 1977 Copernicus Award for "her lifetime achievement as a poet and for her contribution to poetry as a cultural force." This poem, "Evening Plaza, San Miguel," was published in the volume *Beast in View*, 1944.

EVENING PLAZA, SAN MIGUEL

No one will ever understand that evening
Who has not lain the night with a changeable lover,
Changeable as that last evening.

No one who has not ever seen that color
Change and travel the hills, the irrelevant bells
Ringing the changes,

And seen the green enter the evening sky,
Reluctant yellow come and the cathedral
Unfold in rose—

And stood under that rose of stone, remembering rose
Spattered in feasts of rockets, interrupted
By the black downdrawn line

Of the down-turning wheel of carnival—will ever know
The evening color filtered through cinnamon
And how the birds came down

Through the bars of yellow and the bars of green
Into the brandy dusk and the leaves of night,
A touch, a shadow of touch, when breasts

Lift their little branches, and showers and flares of fire
Rise in the blood, in spite of the word of war,
In spite of evening coming down like a lover,

Like the birds falling among the trees, like music
As the trees close, and the cathedral closes.
No one will know who in a stranger land
Has never stood while night came down
In shadows of roses, a cloud of tree-drawn birds,
And said, "I must go home."

RAY BRADBURY

(1 9 2 0 –)

Over the years Ray Bradbury has written more than five hundred stories, poems, essays, plays, films, television plays, radio dramas, music, and even comic books. He's best known for the novels *The Martian Chronicles* (1950) and *Fahrenheit 451* (1953). Bradbury also had the distinct honor of an Apollo astronaut naming the Dandelion Crater after his novel *Dandelion Wine*.

Bradbury was born in Waukegan, Illinois, a place he later fictionalized as "Greentown." After moving back and forth between Illinois and Tucson, Bradbury's family moved to Los Angeles in 1934. Early in his writing career, he traveled to Mexico to collect Indian masks for the Los Angeles County Museum. In the story "Calling Mexico," an old man dying in a small town in Illinois longs to hear one more time the sounds of the city he knew in his younger years.

CALLING MEXICO

And then there is that day when all around, all around you hear the dropping of the apples, one by one, from the trees. At first it is one here and one there, and then it is three and then it is four and then nine and twenty, until the apples plummet like rain, fall like horse hoofs in the soft, darkening grass, and you are the last apple on the tree; and you wait for the wind to work you slowly free from your hold upon the sky, and drop you down and down. Long before you hit the grass you will have forgotten there ever was a tree, or other apples, or a summer, or green grass below. You will fall in darkness. . . .

"No!"

Colonel Freeleigh opened his eyes quickly, sat erect in his wheelchair. He jerked his cold hand out to find the telephone. It was still there! He crushed it against his chest for a moment, blinking.

"I don't like that dream," he said to his empty room.

At last, his fingers trembling, he lifted the receiver and called the long-distance operator and gave her a number and waited, watching the bedroom door as if at any moment a plague of sons, daughters, grandsons, nurses, doctors, might swarm in to seize away this last vital luxury he permitted his failing senses. Many days, or was it years, ago, when his heart had thrust like a dagger through his ribs and flesh, he had heard the boys below . . . their names, what were they? Charles, Charlie, Chuck, yes! And Douglas! And Tom! He remembered! Calling his name far down the hall, but the door being locked in their faces, the boys turned away. You can't be excited, the doctor said. No visitors, no visitors, no visitors. And he heard the boys moving across the street, he saw them, he waved. And they waved back. "Colonel . . . Colonel . . ." And now he sat alone with the little gray toad of a heart flopping weakly here or there in his chest from time to time.

"Colonel Freeleigh," said the operator. "Here's your call. Mexico City. Erickson 3899."

And now the faraway but infinitely clear voice:

"*Bueno.*"

"Jorge!" cried the old man.

"*Señor* Freeleigh? Again? This costs money."

"Let it cost! You know what to do."

"*Sí.* The window?"

"The window, Jorge, if you please."

"A moment," said the voice.

And, thousands of miles away, in a southern land, in an office in a building in that land, there was the sound of footsteps retreat-

ing from the phone. The old man leaned forward, gripping the receiver tight to his wrinkled ear that ached with waiting for the next sound.

The raising of a window.

"Ah," sighed the old man.

The sounds of Mexico City on a hot yellow noon rose through the open window into the waiting phone. He could see Jorge standing there holding the mouthpiece out, out into the bright day.

"Señor . . ."

"No, no, please. Let me *listen*."

He listened to the hooting of many metal horns, the squealing of brakes, the calls of vendors selling red-purple bananas and jungle oranges in their stalls. Colonel Freeleigh's feet began to move, hanging from the edge of his wheelchair, making the motions of a man walking. His eyes squeezed tight. He gave a series of immense sniffs, as if to gain the odors of meats hung on iron hooks in sunshine, cloaked with flies like a mantle of raisins; the smell of stone alleys wet with morning rain. He could feel the sun burn his spiny-bearded cheek, and he was twenty-five years old again, walking, walking, looking, smiling, happy to be alive, very much alert, drinking in colors and smells.

A rap on the door. Quickly he hid the phone under his lap robe.

The nurse entered. "Hello," she said. "Have you been good?"

"Yes." The old man's voice was mechanical. He could hardly see. The shock of a simple rap on the door was such that part of him was still in another city, far removed. He waited for his mind to rush home—it must be here to answer questions, act sane, be polite.

"I've come to check your pulse."

"Not now!" said the old man.

"You're not going anywhere, are you?" She smiled.

He looked at the nurse steadily. He hadn't been anywhere in ten years.

"Give me your wrist."

Her fingers, hard and precise, searched for the sickness in his pulse like a pair of calipers.

"What've you been doing to *excite* yourself?" she demanded.

"Nothing."

Her gaze shifted and stopped on the empty phone table. At that instant a horn sounded faintly, two thousand miles away.

She took the receiver from under the lap robe and held it before his face. "Why do you do this to yourself? You promised you wouldn't. That's how you hurt yourself in the first place, isn't it? Getting excited, talking too much. Those boys up here jumping around—"

"They sat quietly and listened," said the colonel. "And I told them things they'd never heard. The buffalo, I told them, the bison. It was worth it. I don't care. I was in a pure fever and I was alive. It doesn't matter if being so alive kills a man; it's better to have the quick fever every time. Now give me that phone. If you won't let the boys come up and sit politely I can at least talk to someone outside the room."

"I'm sorry, Colonel. Your grandson will have to know about this. I prevented his having the phone taken out last week. Now it looks like I'll let him go ahead."

"This is *my* house, my phone. I pay your salary!" he said.

"To make you well, not get you excited." She wheeled his chair across the room. "To bed with you now, young man!"

From bed he looked back at the phone and kept looking at it.

"I'm going to the store for a few minutes," the nurse said. "Just to be sure you don't use the phone again, I'm hiding your wheelchair in the hall."

She wheeled the empty chair out the door. In the downstairs entry, he heard her pause and dial the extension phone.

Was she phoning Mexico City? he wondered. She wouldn't dare!

The front door shut.

He thought of the last week here, alone, in his room, and the secret, narcotic calls across continents, an isthmus, whole jungle countries of rain forest, blue-orchid plateaus, lakes and hills . . . talking . . . talking . . . to Buenos Aires . . . and . . . Lima . . . Rio de Janeiro . . .

He lifted himself in the cool bed. Tomorrow the telephone gone! What a greedy fool he had been! He slipped his brittle ivory legs down from the bed, marveling at their desiccation. They seemed to be things which had been fastened to his body while he slept one night, while his younger legs were taken off and burned in the cellar furnace. Over the years, they had destroyed all of him, removing hands, arms, and legs and leaving him with substitutes as delicate and useless as chess pieces. And now they were tampering with something more intangible—the memory; they were trying to cut the wires which led back into another year.

He was across the room in a stumbling run. Grasping the phone, he took it with him as he slid down the wall to sit upon the floor. He got the long-distance operator, his heart exploding within him, faster and faster, a blackness in his eyes. "Hurry, hurry!"

He waited.

"Bueno?"

"Jorge, we were cut off."

"You must not phone again, *señor*," said the faraway voice. "Your nurse called me. She says you are very ill. I must hang up."

"No, Jorge! Please!" the old man pleaded. "One last time, listen to me. They're taking the phone out tomorrow. I can never call you again."

Jorge said nothing.

The old man went on. "For the love of God, Jorge! For friendship, then, for the old days! You don't know what it means. You're my age, but you can *move*! I haven't moved anywhere in ten years."

He dropped the phone and had trouble picking it up, his chest was so thick with pain. "Jorge! You *are* still there, aren't you?"

"This will be the last time?" said Jorge.

"I promise!"

The phone was laid on a desk thousands of miles away. Once more, with that clear familiarity, the footsteps, the pause, and, at last, the raising of the window.

"Listen," whispered the old man to himself.

And he heard a thousand people in another sunlight, and the faint, tinkling music of an organ grinder playing "La Marimba"— oh, a lovely, dancing tune.

With eyes tight, the old man put up his hand as if to click pictures of an old cathedral, and his body was heavier with flesh, younger, and he felt the hot pavement underfoot.

He wanted to say, "You're still there, aren't you? All of you people in that city in the time of the early siesta, the shops closing, the little boys crying *lotería nacional para hoy!* to sell lottery tickets. You are all there, the people in the city. I can't believe I was ever among you. When you are away from a city it becomes a fantasy. Any town, New York, Chicago, with its people, becomes improbable with distance. Just as I am improbable here, in Illinois, in a small town by a quiet lake. All of us improbable to one another because we are not present to one another. And so it is good to hear the sounds, and know that Mexico City is still there and the people moving and living. . . ."

He sat with the receiver tightly pressed to his ear.

And at last, the clearest, most improbable sound of all—the sound of a green trolley car going around a corner—a trolley burdened with brown and alien and beautiful people, and the sound of other people running and calling out with triumph as they leaped up and swung aboard and vanished around a corner on the shrieking rails and were borne away in the sun-blazed distance to leave only the sound of tortillas frying on the market stoves, or was it merely the ever rising and falling hum and burn of static quivering along two thousand miles of copper wire . . . ?

The old man sat on the floor.

Time passed.

A downstairs door opened slowly. Light footsteps came in, hesitated, then ventured up the stairs. Voices murmured.

"We shouldn't be here!"

"He phoned me, I tell you. He needs visitors bad. We can't let him down."

"He's sick!"

"Sure! But he said to come when the nurse's out. We'll only stay a second, say hello, and . . ."

The door to the bedroom moved wide. The three boys stood looking in at the old man seated there on the floor.

"Colonel Freeleigh?" said Douglas softly.

There was something in his silence that made them all shut up their mouths.

They approached, almost on tiptoe.

Douglas, bent down, disengaged the phone from the old man's now quite cold fingers. Douglas lifted the receiver to his own ear, listened. Above the static he heard a strange, a far, a final sound.

Two thousand miles away, the closing of a window.

JOHN STEINBECK

(1902–68)

John Steinbeck's first three books were not successful, but *Tortilla Flat*, published in 1935, brought him acclaim. He won a Pulitzer Prize in 1940 for *The Grapes of Wrath*, and in 1962 he was awarded the Nobel Prize for Literature. Steinbeck went to Mexico to collect marine life with the freelance biologist Edward F. Ricketts, and the two men collaborated in writing *Sea of Cortez* (1941), a study of the fauna of the Gulf of California. This trip to the Baja Peninsula provided inspiration for Steinbeck's short novel *The Pearl* (1945).

The Pearl is a retelling of a Mexican folktale. A poor fisherman, Kino, along with his wife, Juana, find an extraordinary pearl, but rather than bringing salvation for their sick baby, Coyotito, the pearl becomes a catalyst for greed and envy. The book is set on Mexico's Baja Peninsula, where natives had lived as fishermen until many were killed by diseases brought by Cortés and his men. Once the local pearls were discovered by Europeans, many Spaniards, adventurers, and natives dove for the legendary gems. In his book *The Forgotten Peninsula*, Joseph Wood Krutch wrote, "Down to the second half of the nineteenth century it [the pearl industry] was the chief source of prosperity for La Paz and the pearls were famous enough, it is said, to find their way into the collections of some of the crowned heads of Europe."

The town lay on a broad estuary, its old yellow plastered buildings hugging the beach. And on the beach the white and blue canoes that came from Nayarit were drawn up, canoes preserved for generations by a hard shell-like waterproof plaster whose making was a secret of the fishing people. They were high and graceful canoes with curving bow and stern and a braced section midships where a mast could be stepped to carry a small lateen sail.

The beach was yellow sand, but at the water's edge a rubble of shell and algae took its place. Fiddler crabs bubbled and sputtered in their holes in the sand, and in the shallows little lobsters popped in and out of their tiny homes in the rubble and sand. The sea bottom was rich with crawling and swimming and growing things. The brown algae waved in the gentle currents and the green eel grass swayed and little sea horses clung to its stems. Spotted botete, the poison fish, lay on the bottom in the eel-grass beds, and the bright-colored swimming crabs scampered over them.

On the beach the hungry dogs and the hungry pigs of the town searched endlessly for any dead fish or sea bird that might have floated in on a rising tide.

Although the morning was young, the hazy mirage was up. The uncertain air that magnified some things and blotted out others hung over the whole Gulf so that all sights were unreal and vision could not be trusted; so that sea and land had the sharp clarities and the vagueness of a dream. Thus it might be that the people of the Gulf trust things of the spirit and things of the imagination, but they do not trust their eyes to show them distance or clear outline or any optical exactness. Across the estuary from the town one section of mangroves stood clear and telescopically defined, while another mangrove clump was a hazy black-green blob. Part of the far shore disappeared into a shimmer that looked like water. There was no certainty in seeing, no proof that what you saw was there or was not there. And the people of the Gulf expected all places were that way, and it was not strange to them. A copper haze hung over the water, and the hot morning sun beat on it and made it vibrate blindingly.

The brush houses of the fishing people were back from the beach on the right-hand side of the town, and the canoes were drawn up in front of this area.

Kino and Juana came slowly down to the beach and to Kino's canoe, which was the one thing of value he owned in the world. It was very old. Kino's grandfather had brought it from Nayarit, and he had given it to Kino's father, and so it had come to Kino. It was at once property and source of food, for a man with a boat can guarantee a woman that she will eat something. It is the bulwark against starvation. And every year Kino refinished his canoe with the hard shell-like plaster by the secret method that had also come to him from his father. Now he came to the canoe and touched the bow tenderly as he always did. He laid his diving rock and his basket and the two ropes in the sand by the canoe. And he folded his blanket and laid it in the bow.

Juana laid Coyotito on the blanket, and she placed her shawl over him so that the hot sun could not shine on him. He was quiet now, but the swelling on his shoulder had continued up his neck and under his ear and his face was puffed and feverish. Juana went to the water and waded in. She gathered some brown seaweed and made a flat damp poultice of it, and this she applied to the baby's swollen shoulder, which was as good a remedy as any and probably better than the doctor could have done. But the remedy lacked his authority because it was simple and didn't cost anything. The stomach cramps had not come to Coyotito. Perhaps Juana had sucked out the poison in time, but she had not sucked out her worry over her first-born. She had not prayed directly for the recovery of the baby—she had prayed that they might find a pearl with which to hire the doctor to cure the baby, for the minds of people are as unsubstantial as the mirage of the Gulf.

Now Kino and Juana slid the canoe down the beach to the water, and when the bow floated, Juana climbed in, while Kino pushed the stern in and waded beside it until it floated lightly and trembled on the little breaking waves. Then in co-ordination Juana and Kino drove their double-bladed paddles into the sea, and the canoe creased the water and hissed with speed. The other pearlers were gone out long since. In a few moments Kino could see them clustered in the haze, riding over the oyster bed.

Light filtered down through the water to the bed where the frilly pearl oysters lay fastened to the rubbly bottom, a bottom strewn with shells of broken, opened oysters. This was the bed that had raised the King of Spain to be a great power in Europe in past years, had helped to pay for his wars, and had decorated the churches for his soul's sake. The gray oysters with ruffles like skirts on the shells, the barnacle-crusted oysters with little bits of weed clinging to the skirts and small crabs climbing over them. An accident could happen to these oysters, a grain of sand could lie in the folds of muscle and irritate the flesh until in self-protection the flesh coated the grain with a layer of smooth cement. But once started, the flesh continued to coat the foreign body until it fell free in some tidal flurry or until the oyster was destroyed. For centuries men had dived down and torn the oysters from the beds and ripped them open, looking for the coated grains of sand. Swarms of fish lived near the bed to live near the oysters thrown back by the searching men and to nibble at the shining inner shells. But the pearls were accidents, and the finding of one was luck, a little pat on the back by God or the gods or both.

Kino had two ropes, one tied to a heavy stone and one to a basket. He stripped off his shirt and trousers and laid his hat in the bottom of the canoe. The water was oily smooth. He took his rock in one hand and his basket in the other, and he slipped feet first over the side and the rock carried him to the bottom. The bubbles rose behind him until the water cleared and he could see. Above, the surface of the water was an undulating mirror of brightness, and he could see the bottoms of the canoes sticking through it.

Kino moved cautiously so that the water would not be obscured with mud or sand. He hooked his foot in the loop on his rock and his hands worked quickly, tearing the oysters loose, some singly, others in clusters. He laid them in his basket. In some places the oysters clung to one another so that they came free in lumps.

Now, Kino's people had sung of everything that happened or existed. They had made songs to the fishes, to the sea in anger and to the sea in calm, to the light and the dark and the sun and the moon, and the songs were all in Kino and in his people—every song that had ever been made, even the ones forgotten. And as he filled his basket the song was in Kino, and the beat of the song was his pounding heart as it ate the oxygen from his held breath, and the melody of the song was the gray-green water and the little scuttling animals and the clouds of fish that flitted by and were gone. But in the song there was a secret little inner song, hardly perceptible, but always there, sweet and secret and clinging, almost hiding in the counter-melody, and this was the Song of the Pearl That Might Be, for every shell thrown in the basket might contain a pearl. Chance was against it, but luck and the gods might be for it. And in the canoe above him Kino knew that Juana was making the magic of prayer, her face set rigid and her muscles hard to force the luck, to tear the luck out of the gods' hands, for she needed the luck for the swollen shoulder of Coyotito. And because the need was great and the desire was great, the little secret melody of the pearl that might be was stronger this morning. Whole phrases of it came clearly and softly into the Song of the Undersea.

Kino, in his pride and youth and strength, could remain down over two minutes without strain, so that he worked deliberately, selecting the largest shells. Because they were disturbed, the oyster shells were tightly closed. A little to his right a hummock of rubbly rock stuck up, covered with young oysters not ready to take. Kino moved next to the hummock, and then, beside it, under a little overhang, he saw a very large oyster lying by itself, not covered with its clinging brothers. The shell was partly open, for the overhang protected this ancient oyster, and in the lip-like muscle Kino saw a ghostly gleam, and then the shell closed down. His heart beat out a heavy rhythm and the melody of the maybe pearl shrilled in his ears. Slowly he forced the oyster loose and held it tightly against his breast. He kicked his foot free from the rock loop, and his body rose to the surface and his black hair gleamed in the sunlight. He reached over the side of the canoe and laid the oyster in the bottom.

Then Juana steadied the boat while he climbed in. His eyes were shining with excitement, but in decency he pulled up his rock, and then he pulled up his basket of oysters and lifted them in. Juana sensed his excitement, and she pretended to look away. It is not good to want a thing too much. It sometimes drives the luck away. You must want it just enough, and you must be very tactful with God or the gods. But Juana stopped breathing. Very deliberately Kino opened his short strong knife. He looked speculatively at the basket. Perhaps it would be better to open *the* oyster last. He took a small oyster from the basket, cut the muscle, searched the folds of flesh, and threw it in the water. Then he seemed to see the great oyster for the first time. He squatted in the bottom of the canoe, picked up the shell and examined it. The flutes were shining black to brown, and only a few small barnacles adhered to the shell. Now Kino was reluctant to open it. What he had seen, he knew, might be a reflection, a piece of flat shell accidently drifted in or a complete illusion. In this Gulf of uncertain light there were more illusions than realities.

But Juana's eyes were on him and she could not wait. She put her hand on Coyotito's covered head. "Open it," she said softly.

Kino deftly slipped his knife into the edge of the shell. Through the knife he could feel the muscle tighten hard. He worked the blade lever-wise and the closing muscle parted and the shell fell apart. The lip-like flesh writhed up and then subsided. Kino lifted the flesh, and there it lay, the great pearl, perfect as the moon. It captured the light and refined it and gave it back in silver incandescence. It was as large as a sea-gull's egg. It was the greatest pearl in the world.

LUIS RODRIGUEZ

(1954–)

Luis Rodriguez is an award-winning poet, journalist, essayist, children's book writer, memoirist, short story writer, and novelist. His novel, *Music of the Mill*, was published in 2005, and his latest book of poetry is *My Nature is Hunger: New and Selected Poems* (2005). He is also a cofounder of Tia Chucha's Cafe & Centro Cultural, a multiarts, multimedia bookstore/cafe/cultural center in the San Fernando Valley section of Los Angeles. Rodriguez is perhaps best known for his memoir, *Always Running: La Vida Loca—Gang Days in L.A.*, about his childhood. His family left Chihuahua, Mexico, first for El Paso, then Los Angeles. Rodriguez decided to document his youth as an East Los Angeles gang member in an effort to steer his teenaged son away from the gang that he had recently joined.

This poem, "The Old Woman of Mérida," from his latest book of poems, is quite different from his gritty social commentary. It's an intimate and sensual view of an old woman who still lives by the sea that made her a widow.

THE OLD WOMAN OF MÉRIDA

The old woman stares out an open window,
shards of sunlight pierce her face
cutting shadows on skin. She is washing
her hands after the dishes, dipping them
into a sea of hues and shapes,
a sea of syllables without sound,
in a stone house in Mérida,
her Mérida of dense Mexico.

The water is a view to a distant place:
Kitchen walls fall to reveal a gray sky,
an array of birds in flight through fog
—the crushed white of waves curling at feet.
There appears a woman in forested hair,
eyes of black pearl,
who touches the hewn face of a man
and palms that feel like bark.
She cringes at its blemishes
and something in her careens
against the walls of her heart.
She never wants to let go,
never wants to stop tracing
the scars above his eyebrows,
the tattoos on blackened skin,
while the lick of a tongue
stirs the night inside her.

The old woman looks at water and into
this vision shaped into a mouth
—the mouth of the sea that swallowed
her sailor-husband,
so many sunlit windows ago.

SIGHTS, SOUNDS, AND TASTES

Fiesta del Pueblo

FRANCES CALDERÓN DE LA BARCA

(1804–82)

Scots-born Frances Erskine Inglis first met Don Angel Calderón de la Barca in New York City when he worked as Spanish minister to the United States and she was a Staten Island schoolteacher. They married, and in 1839, when he was appointed the first Spanish minister to a newly independent Mexico, she accompanied him and lived there for two years. She embraced her time there, traveling widely throughout the country. Her observations in letters and journals of local food, nature, the social elite of Mexico City, and the bandits along the highways were published in her book, *Life in Mexico*. This personal travel guide blended with historical facts proves a lively and still relevant read today.

In the following passage, she describes the floating gardens just south of Mexico City, now known by the Aztec Xochimilco, or "garden of flowers." This area was once the agricultural hub of Tenochtitlán, the capital of the Aztec Empire. To cultivate crops, the Aztecs created "chinampas," or raised agricultural fields in the lake. These resulted in a series of canals in the lake where, centuries later, gondola-type boats are punted along between beds of flowers, while mariachi musicians serenade. The flowers and music Calderón de la Barca described a century and a half ago are still abundantly in evidence.

Though there is very little going on in Mexico at present, I amuse myself very well; there is so much to see, and the people are so kind and friendly. Having got riding horses we have been making excursions all round the country, especially early in the morning, before the sun is high, when the air is delightfully cool and refreshing. Sometimes we go to the Viga at six in the morning, to see the Indians bringing in their flowers and vegetables by the canal. The profusion of sweet-peas, double poppies, bluebottles, stock gillyflower, and roses, I never saw equalled. Each Indian woman in her canoe looks as if seated in a floating flower-garden. The same love of flowers distinguishes them now as in the time of Cortés; the same which Humboldt remarked centuries afterwards. In the evening these Indian women, in their canoes, are constantly crowned with garlands of roses or poppies. Those who sit in the market, selling their fruit or their vegetables, appear as if they sat in bowers formed of fresh green branches and coloured flowers. In the poorest village-church the floor is strewed with flowers, and before the service begins fresh nosegays are brought in and arranged upon the altar. The baby at its christening, the bride at the altar, the dead body in its bier, are all adorned with flowers. We are told that in the days of Cortés a bouquet of rare flowers was the most valuable gift presented to the ambassadors who visited the court of Montezuma, and it presents a strange anomaly, this love of flowers having existed along with their sanguinary worship and barbarous sacrifices.

We went the other evening on the canal, in a large canoe with an awning, as far as the little village of Santa Anita, and saw, for the first time, the far-famed Chinampas, or floating gardens, which have now become fixtures, and are covered with vegetables, intermingled with flowers, with a few poor huts beside them, occupied by the Indians, who bring these to the city for sale. There were cauliflowers, chili, tomatoes, cabbages, and other vegetables, but I was certainly disappointed in their beauty. They are however curious, on account of their origin. So far back as 1245, it is said the wandering Aztecs or Mexicans arrived first at Chapultepec, when, being persecuted by the princes of Taltocan, they took refuge in a group of islands to the south of the lake of Tezcuco. Falling under the yoke of the Tezcucan kings, they abandoned their island home and fled to Tezapan, where, as a reward for assisting the chiefs of that country in a war against other petty princes, they received their freedom, and established themselves in a city to which they gave the name of Mexicalsingo, from Mejitli, their god of war—now a collection of strong barns and poor huts. But they did not settle there, for to obey an oracle they transported themselves from this city to the islands east of Chapultepec to the western side of the lake of Tezcuco. An ancient tradition had long been current amongst them, that wherever they should behold an eagle seated upon a nopal whose roots pierced a rock, there they should found a great city. In 1325 they beheld this sign, and on the spot, in an island in the lake, founded the first house of God—the Teocalli, or Great Temple of Mexico. During all their wanderings, wherever they stopped, the Aztecs cultivated the earth, and lived upon what nature gave them. Surrounded by enemies and in the midst of a lake where there are few fish, necessity and industry compelled them to form floating fields and gardens on the bosom of the waters.

They weaved together the roots of aquatic plants, intertwined with twigs and light branches, until they had formed a foundation sufficiently strong to support a soil formed of the earth which they drew from the bottom of the lake; and on it they sowed their maize, their chili, and all other plants necessary for their support. These floating gardens were about a foot above the water, and in the form of a long square. Afterwards, in their natural taste for flowers, they not only cultivated the useful but the ornamental, and these small gardens multiplying were covered with flowers and aromatic herbs, which were used in the worship of the gods, or were sent to ornament the palace of the emperor. The Chinampas along the canal of the Viga are no longer floating gardens, but fixed to the main land in the marshy grounds lying between the two great lakes of Chalco and Tezcuco. A small trench full of water separates each garden; and though now in this marshy land they give but a faint idea of what they may have been when they raised their flower-crowned heads above the clear waters of the lake, and when the Indians, in their barks, wishing to remove their habitations, could tow along their little islands of roses, it is still a pretty and a pleasant scene.

We bought numerous garlands of roses and poppies from the Indian children, both here and at Santa Anita, a little village where we landed, and as we returned towards evening we were amused by the singing and dancing of the Indians. One canoe came close up to ours, and kept beside it for some time. A man was lying lazily at the bottom of the boat tingling his guitar, and one or two women were dancing monotonously and singing at the same time to his music. Sundry jars of pulque and earthen dishes with tortillas and chili and pieces of *tasajo*, long festoons of dried and salted beef, proved that the party were not without their solid comforts, in spite of the romantic guitar and the rose and poppy garlands with which the dancing nymphs were crowned. Amongst others they performed the *Palomo*, the Dove, one of their most favourite dances. The music is pretty, and I send it you with the words, the music from ear; the words are given me by my friend the Señora A——d, who sings all these little Indian airs in perfection. If we may form some judgment of a people's civilization by their ballads, none of the Mexican songs give us a very high idea of theirs. The words are generally a tissue of absurdities, nor are there any patriotic songs which their new-born freedom might have called forth from so musical a people. At least I have as yet only discovered one air of which the words bear reference to the glorious "Grito de Dolores," and which asserts in rhyme that on account of that memorable event, the Indian was able to get as drunk as a Christian! The translation of the Palomo is as follows:

"What are you doing, little dove, there in the wine-shop? Waiting for my love until Tuesday, my life. A dove in flying hurt her little wing. If you have your dove I have my little dove too. A dove in flying all her feathers fell off. Women pay badly; not all, but some of them. Little dove of the barracks, you will tell the drummers when they beat the retreat to strike up the march of my loves. Little dove, what are you doing there leaning against that wall? Waiting for my dove till he brings me something to eat." At the end of each verse the chorus of "Palomita, palomo, palomo."

Yet, monotonous as it is, the air is so pretty, the women sang so softly and sleepily, the music sounded so soothingly as we glided along the water, that I felt in a pleasant half-dreamy state of perfect contentment, and was sorry when arriving at the landing-place, we had to return to a carriage and civilized life, with nothing but the garlands of flowers to remind us of the Chinampas.

Unfortunately these people generally end by too frequent applications to the jarro of pulque, or what is worse to the pure spirit known by the name of *chinguirite*; the consequence of which is, that from music and dancing and rose-becrowning, they proceed to quarrelling and jealousy and drunkenness, which frequently terminates in their fighting, stabbing each other, or throwing each other into the canal. "The end crowns the work."

Noble as this present city of Mexico is one cannot help thinking how much more picturesque the ancient Tenochtitlán was, and how much more fertile its valley must have been, on account of the great lakes. Yet even in the time of Cortés these lakes had no great depth of water, and still further back, in the time of the Indian emperors, navigation had been so frequently interrupted in seasons of drought, that an aqueduct had been constructed in order to supply the canals with water.

After this, the Spaniards, like all new settlers, hewed down the fine trees in this beautiful valley, both on plain and mountain, leaving the bare soil exposed to the vertical rays of the sun. Then their well-founded dread of inundation caused them to construct the famous *Desagüe* of Huehuetoca, the drain or subterranean conduit or channel in the mountain for drawing off the waters of the lakes, thus leaving marshy lands or sterile plains covered with carbonate of soda, where formerly were silver lakes covered with canoes. This last was a necessary evil, since the Indian emperors themselves were sensible of its necessity and had formed great works for draining the lakes, some remains of which works still exist in the vicinity of the Penon. The great Desagüe was begun in 1607, when the Marquis of Salinas was viceroy of Mexico; and the operations were commenced with great pomp, the viceroy assisting in person, mass being said on a portable altar, and fifteen hundred workmen assembled, while the marquis himself began the excavation by giving the first stroke with a spade. From 1607 to 1830, eight millions of dollars were expended, and yet this great work was not brought to a conclusion. However, the limits of the two lakes of Zumpango and San Cristobal, to the north of the valley, were thus greatly reduced, and the lake of Tezcuco, the most beautiful of all the five, no longer received their contributions. Thus the danger of inundations has diminished, but water and vegetation have diminished also, and the suburbs of the city, which were formerly covered with beautiful gardens, now present to the eye an arid expanse of efflorescent salt. The plains near San Lazaro especially, in their arid whiteness, seem characteristic of the unfortunate victims of leprosy enclosed in the walls of that hospital.

We rode out the other day by the *barrio*, or ward of Santiago, which occupies part of the ancient Tlatelolco, which once constituted a separate state, had kings of its own, and was conquered by a Mexican monarch, who made a communication by bridges between it and Mexico. The great market mentioned by Cortés was held here, and its boundaries are still pointed out, whilst the convent chapel stands on the height where Cortés erected a battering engine, when he was besieging the Indian Venice.

FANNY CHAMBERS GOOCH INGLEHART

(1 8 4 2 – 1 9 1 3)

The full title of the book from which this excerpt is drawn is *Face to Face with the Mexicans: The Domestic Life, Educational, Social, and Business Ways, Statesmanship and Literature, Legendary and General History of the Mexican People, as seen and studied by an American woman during seven years of intercourse with them* (1887). Its author was born in Hillsboro, Mississippi, was educated in Texas, and for a while studied in France. She loved to travel, and married three times; it was with her husband G. W. Gooch that she traveled to Mexico. They lived in an adobe house in Saltillo, where Fanny learned Spanish and decided to help her fellow countrymen in the States understand Mexicans. With this goal in mind, she traveled widely and wrote her impressions, describing religious festivities and holiday activities, rituals such as baptism and marriage, along with recipes and popular stories. In the following excerpt she describes the *posada* celebrated in Mexico City.

A Mexican Christmas is very unlike one in the United States. No merry jingle of sleigh-bells is heard in this sunny land where the rigors of winter are unknown, and the few lofty peaks, where alone snow is ever seen, would hardly tempt the most adventurous tobogganist.

As there are no chimneys, Santa Claus is deprived of his legitimate and time-honored entrance into households, so the delightful and immemorial custom of hanging up stockings is unknown to Mexican children. But perhaps they enjoy themselves quite as much after their own fashion as ours do. One circumstance in their favor is the long-continued celebration, which, beginning on the evening of the 17th of December and continuing till New-Year's Day, is one long, delightful jubilee.

The celebrations in honor of Guadalupe extend from the 12th until the *posadas*, or nine days' festivities. The last prayers on the lips of the faithful and the last tones from organ and choir in praise of the patron saint, hardly die away ere the Christmas rejoicings begin.

The world *posada* signifies an inn, and the whole observance is a relic bequeathed by the Spaniards. The celebration is limited almost exclusively to the capital and the larger cities, and may be considered more as a social feature than belonging specially to the Church—though really combining the elements of both.

It is a reminder of the Nativity, based on the Gospel narrative, but with additions. When Caesar Augustus issued the decree that "all the world should be taxed," the Virgin and Joseph came from Galilee to Judea to enroll their names for taxation. Bethlehem, their city, was so full of people from all parts of the world that they wandered about for nine days, without finding admittance in either hotel or private house. As nothing better offered, they at last took refuge in a manger, where the Saviour was born.

The first act of the *posada* represents the journey of the Virgin Mary and Joseph from Nazareth to Bethlehem, and the difficulties they experienced in finding shelter. The family and invited guests march in procession through halls and around corridors, holding in their hands lighted tapers and singing solemn litanies. Before the procession, the figures of Mary and Joseph are borne along by servants or young boys. Each door they pass is knocked upon, but no answer or invitation to enter is given, and so the procession continues to move around, singing and knocking, until, at last, a door is opened, when they all enter and mass is said and hymns are sung with all possible solemnity, after which the other interesting features of the *posada* are presented, as hereafter related.

Sometimes a *burro* is introduced to represent the faithful animal that carried the holy family in their journeyings.

All over the city is heard the litany of the *posadas*, sung in a hundred homes, as the pilgrimages wind in and out of the rooms and round the improvised shrines. Venetian lights hang in the *patios*, and fireworks blaze skyward in every direction. One of the most interesting features is the infantile resort set up in the southern part of the plaza. The Zócalo is a bewitching place; lights flash through the branches of pine and cypress, and the place is alive with children of the first families of Mexico.

The breaking of the *piñata* is the chief sport of the *posada*. The *piñata* is an oval-shaped, earthen jar, handsomely decorated and covered with bright ornaments, tinsel, gay flowers, and flaunting streamers of tissue paper. The common people are experts in the manufacture of these curious objects, and when a vender of them is seen perambulating the streets, it is worth while stopping to examine his stock in trade. There are turkeys, horses, birds, monkeys—in fact, every beast, bird or fowl of the air that is known. In addition, there are children almost life-sized, and even brides, with the trained dress, veil and orange blossoms. But oh! the hapless fate of these earthen brides! They are soon beaten and smashed into atoms by the fun-loving crowd.

The holy figures are left in the chapel after the litanies are ended, and then, either in the *patio* or a room selected for the purpose, the fun of breaking the *piñata* begins. It is suspended from the ceiling, and each person desiring to take part is, in turn, blindfolded. Armed with a long pole, he proceeds to strike the swinging *piñata*. Often a dozen people are blindfolded before the final crash comes, and the *dulces* go rattling over the floor. Then such racing and chasing!

The first *posada* that I attended was impromptu without the procession, litany, or Mary and Joseph; the *piñata* was a monkey, and my young Mexican friends insisted I should be the one to break it. Being duly blindfolded, and armed with a long pole, while the crowd of Spanish-speaking people looked on, asserting that I could and would not fail in the effort, I set confidently about my task. But no sound came of broken crockery or falling *dulces*.

The rule was, that every one should have three trials. After the third stroke imagine my chagrin, when the handkerchief was removed, to see the monkey above my head, slowly descending, grinning and wriggling his tail. A wild and clamorous burst of laughter went up when I discovered the trick. They insisted that I should have another stroke at his monkeyship; so, acting on the rule, "If at first you don't succeed," blindfolded and pole in hand, I advanced, and, with one vigorous stroke, shivered it, amid shouts of laughter and rounds of applause. No *dulces* were ever so sweet to me!

CHARLES MACOMB FLANDRAU

(1871–1938)

Charles Macomb Flandrau, born in St. Paul, Minnesota, made his mark early as a writer with *Harvard Episodes*, a series of vignettes about the life and high jinks of Harvard students. Although financially independent, from 1899 to 1902 Flandrau contributed to the *Saturday Evening Post*. In 1908 he wrote a book called *Viva Mexico!*, an account of time spent on his brother's coffee plantation in Chiapas, Mexico. Although he showed much early promise as a writer, he later wrote very little except theater reviews and letters to friends.

Flandrau's *Viva Mexico!* is still considered a classic travel book and his detailed account of coffee farming illuminates this involved process. In recent years, more attention has been paid to coffee farming in Chiapas from an environmental perspective, as shade-grown, ecologically sensitive coffee is becoming popular not only for its quality, but for providing natural habitat to migrating birds and butterflies. Coffee farming has become political, as indigenous people involved in the Zapatista uprising of 1994 have formed coffee cooperatives to stimulate economic prospects in this poor but beautiful state. In *Viva Mexico!* Flandrau refers to the work of his predecessor, Frances Calderón de la Barca: "what strikes me as significant when I open Madame Calderón's letters at random and read a page or two almost anywhere is that, while the book has long since been out of print, it is essentially not out of date." The same can be said about *Viva Mexico!*

Here is a letter from a coffee plantation:

When I got back in October, they received me with formalities—gave me a kind of Roman triumph. If it hadn't been so pathetic I should have laughed; if it hadn't been so funny I should have cried. For I had been fourteen hours on a slow-climbing mule, and you know—or rather you don't know—how the last interminable two hours of that kind of riding unstrings one. Being Mexican, everything about the Roman triumph went wrong and fell perfectly flat. In the first place they expected me a day earlier, and when I didn't arrive they decided—Heaven knows why— that I wouldn't come the next day, but the day after. In the meanwhile I appeared late in the afternoon of the day between. They had built in front of the piazza a wobbly arch of great glossy leaves and red flowers, and from post to post had hung chains of red, white, and green tissue paper. But the arch, of course, had blown down in the night and most of the paper garlands had been rained on and were hanging limply to the posts. All this, they assured me, would have been repaired had I arrived a day later, and I marveled at my self-control as I enthusiastically admired the beauty of a welcoming arch lying prostrate in the mud.

It had been the pleasant intention of everyone to assemble and welcome me home, and when at the entrance to the ranch the Indian who lives there gave a prolonged, falsetto cry (un grito)— the signal agreed on—and I rode up the slope to the clanging of the bell we ring to call in the pickers, and the detonations of those terrible Mexican rockets that give no light but rend the sky apart, I had a feeling as of a concourse awaiting me. The concourse, however, had given me up until the next day, and when I got off my mule I found that the entire festivities were being conducted by Manuel the house-boy, Rosalía the cook, the Trinidad the may-ordomo. Trinidad shot off all six cartridges in his revolver and then shook hands with me. Rosalía was attached to the bell rope—Manuel was manipulating the rockets. At that moment I knew exactly how the hero feels when the peasantry (no doubt such plays are now extinct) exclaims: "The young squire comes of age to-day. Hurray, hurray, hurray! There will be great doings up at the hall. Hurray, hurray, hurray!" It was all so well meant that when I went into my bedroom I could not bring myself to scold at what I found there. On the clean, brown cedar walls they had pasted pictures—advertisements of sewing machines and breakfast foods and automobiles, cut from the back pages of magazines and slapped on anywhere. They see but few pictures, and ours, although rather meaningless to them, are fascinating. A picture is a picture, and my walls were covered with them; but I pretended to be greatly pleased. Since then I have been quietly soaking them off at the tactful rate of about two a week.

Trinidad, the new mayordomo, seems to have done well in my absence. He planted thirty-five thousand new coffee trees with an intelligence positively human. Casimiro, his predecessor, and I parted last year—not in anger, only in sorrow. Casimiro had been a highwayman—a bandit. His police record, they say, makes creepy reading on dark and windy nights. That, however, I never took in consideration. It was only when he began to gamble and to make good his losses by selling me my own corn and pocketing the money that we bade each other good-by. There was no scene. When I told him such things could not go on, he gravely agreed with me that they couldn't, and without resentment departed the next morning. They are strange people. When they do lose control of themselves they go to any lengths; there is likely to be a scene more than worth the price of admission. Somebody usually gets killed. But nothing short of this would seem to be, as a rule, worth while, and on the surface their manner is one of indifference— detachment. Trinidad, who took Casimiro's place, rose, so to speak, from the ranks. He was an arriero for seven years and then drifted here as a day laborer. But he understands coffee, and the experiment of suddenly placing him over all the others has so far been a success.

What a watchful eye the authorities keep on them even in far-away places like this! The instant Trinidad ceased to be a common laborer on whatever he could earn a day by picking coffee, hauling firewood, cleaning the trees, and received a salary of thirty-five pesos a month, his taxes were raised. They all pay a monthly tax (the "contribución" it is called) of a few centavos, although what most of them, owning absolutely nothing, are taxed for, it would be hard to say, unless it be for breathing the air of heaven—for being alive at all. He tried to keep secret the fact of his advancement, but it became known of course, and his tax, to his great disgust, was raised fifteen or twenty cents.

Last week we had our first picking of the year and, weather permitting (which it won't be), we shall pick with more or less continuity for the next four months. Coffee is different from other crops ("not like other girls") and often inclines me to believe it has acquired some of its characteristics from prolonged and intimate contact with the hands that pick it. For quite in the Mexican manner it cannot bring itself to do anything so definite and thorough as to ripen—like wheat or corn or potatoes—all at once. A few berries turn red on every tree and have to be removed before they fall off. By the time this has been done from one end of the place to the other, more have ripened and reddened and the pickers begin again. "Poco a poco—not to-day shall we be ready for you, but to-morrow, or perhaps next week. To do anything so final—in fact, to be ready on any specific date is not the custom of the country," the trees seem to say. However, it is just as well. Nature apparently knew what she was doing. To pick the berries properly requires skill and time, and if they all ripened at once one could not take care of them.

Beyond the fact that you "don't take sugar, thank you," and like to have the cream poured in first, do you know anything about coffee? Did you know that the pretty, fussy trees (they are really more like large shrubs) won't grow in the sun and won't grow in the shade, but have to be given companionship in the form of other trees that, high above them, permit just enough and not too much sunlight to filter mildly in? And that unless you twist off the berries in a persuasive, almost gentle fashion, you so hurt their feelings that in the spring they may refuse to flower? And that the branches are so brittle, they have a way of cracking off from the weight of their own crop? And that wherever there is coffee there is also a tough, graceful little vine about as thick as a telegraph wire which, if left uncut, winds itself around and around a tree, finally strangling it to death as a snake strangles a rabbit?

When I see the brown hands of the pickers fluttering like nimble birds among the branches, and think of the eight patient processes to which the little berries must be subjected before they can become a cup of drinkable coffee, I often wonder how and by whom their secret was wrested from them. Was it an accident like the original whitening of sugar, when—so we used to be told—a chicken with clay on its feet ran over a mound of crude, brown crystals? Or did a dejected Arabian, having heard all his life that (like the tomato of our grandmothers') it was a deadly thing, attempt by drinking it to assuage forever a hopeless passion for some bulbul of the desert, and then find himself not dead, but waking? A careless woman drops a bottle of bluing into a vat of wood pulp and lo! for the first time we have colored writing paper. But no one ever inadvertently picked, dispulped, fermented, washed, dried, hulled, roasted, ground, and boiled coffee, and unless most of these things are done to it, it is of no possible use.

After the coffee is picked it is brought home in sacks, measured, and run through the dispulper, a machine that removes the tough red, outer skin. Every berry (except the pea berry—a freak) is composed of two beans, and these are covered with a sweet, slimy substance known as the "honey," which has to ferment and rot before the beans may be washed. Washing simply removes the honey and those pieces of the outer skin that have escaped the teeth of the machine and flowed from the front end where they weren't wanted. Four or five changes of water are made in the course of the operation, and toward the last, when the rotted honey has been washed away, leaving the beans hard and clean in their coverings of parchment, one of the men takes off his trousers, rolls up his drawers, and knee deep in the heavy mixture of coffee and water drags his feet as rapidly as he can around the cement washing tank until the whole mass is in motion with a swirling eddy in the center. Into the eddy gravitate all the impurities—the foreign substances—the dead leaves and twigs and unwelcome hulls, and when they all seem to be there, the man deftly scoops them up with his hands and tosses them over the side. Then, if it be a fine hot day, the soggy mess is shoveled on the asoleadero (literally, the sunning place), an immense sloping stone platform covered with smooth cement, and there it is spread out to dry while men in their bare feet constantly turn it over with wooden hoes in order that the beans may receive the sun equally on all sides.

It sounds simple, and if one numbered among one's employees a Joshua who could command the sun to stand still when one wished it to, it doubtless would be. But no matter how much coffee there may be spread out on the asoleadero, the sun not only loses its force at a certain hour and then inconsiderately sets, it sometimes refuses for weeks at a time to show itself at all. During these dreary eternities the half-dried coffee is stowed away in sacks or, when it is too wet to dispose of in this manner without danger of molding, it is heaped up in ridges on the asoleadero and covered. When it rains, work of all kinds in connection with the coffee necessarily ceases. The dryers cannot dry and the pickers cannot pick. Even when it is not actually raining the pickers won't go out if the trees are still wet. For the water from the shaken branches chills and stiffens their bloodless hands and soaks through their cotten clothes to the skin. If one's plantation and one's annual crop are large enough to justify the expense, one may defy the sun by investing in what is known as a secadero—a machine for drying coffee by artificial heat. But I haven't arrived at one of these two-thousand-dollar sun-scorners—yet.

That is as far as I go with my coffee—I pick it, dispulp it, wash it, dry it, and sell it. But while the first four of these performances sometimes bid fair to worry me into my grave before my prime, and the fourth at least is of vital importance, as the flavor of coffee may certainly be marred, if not made, in the drying, they are but the prelude to what is eventually done to it before you critically sip it and declare it to be good or bad. Women and children pick it over by hand, separating it into different classes; it is then run through one machine that divests it of its parchment covering; another, with the uncanny precision of mindless things, gropes for beans that happen to be of exactly the same shape, wonderfully finds them, and drops them into their respective places; while at the same time it is throwing out every bean that either nature or the dispulping machine has in the slightest degree mutilated. The sensitiveness and apperception of this iron and wooden box far exceed my own. Often I am unable to see the difference between the beans it has chosen to disgorge into one sack and the beans it has relegated to another—to feel the justice of its irrevocable decisions. But they are always just, and every bean it drops into the defective sack will be found, on examination, to be defective. Then there is still another machine for polishing the bean—rubbing off the delicate, tissue-paper membrane that covers it inside of the parchment. This process does not affect the flavor. In fact nothing affects the flavor of coffee after it has once been dried; but the separation and the polishing give it what is known to the trade as "style." And in the trade there is as much poppycock about coffee as there is about wine and cigars. When you telephone to your grocer for a mixture of Mocha and Java do you by any chance imagine that you are going to receive coffee from Arabia and the Dutch islands? What you do receive, the coffee kings alone know. There are, I have been told, a few sacks of real Mocha in the United States, just as there are a few real Vandykes and Holbeins, and if you are very lucky indeed, the Mocha in your mixture will have been grown in Mexico.

Sometimes at the height of the picking season the day is not long enough, the washing tanks are not large enough, and the workers are not numerous enough to attend to both the coffee-drying on the asoleadero and the growing pile of berries that are constantly being carried in from the trees. When this happens the dispulping has to be done at night, and until four or five in the morning the monotonous plaint of the machine, grinding, grinding like the mills of some insatiable Mexican god, comes faintly over from the tanks. Under a flaring torch and fortified with a bottle of aguardiente the men take turns through the long night at filling the hopper and turning the heavy wheel, bursting now and then into wild, improvised recitatives that are answered by whomever happens for the moment to be most illuminated by either the aguardiente or the divine fire. They begin to improvise to this rapid, savage burst of a few minor phrases from the time they are children. Almost any grown man can do it, although there is a standard of excellence in the art (I have begun to detect it when I hear it), recognized among themselves, that only a few attain. It takes into consideration both the singer's gift for dramatic or lyric invention and the quality of his voice, a loud, strained tenor with falsetto embellishments being the most desirable. I have heard Censio, the mayordomo's little boy, aged three or four, singing, for an hour at a time, sincere and simple eulogies of his father's cows. Since I brought him a small patrol wagon drawn by two spirited iron horses his voice, however, is no longer lifted in commemoration of "O mis vacas! O mis vacas! O mis vacas!" but of "O mis caballitos! O mis caballitos! O mis caballitos!" They improvise, too, at the dances, where the music is usually a harp and a jarana—breaking in anywhere, saying their say, and then waiting for the reply. Women rarely take part in these Tannhäuseresque diversions, although I remember one woman at a dance on my own piazza who got up and proceeded to chant with a wealth of personal and rather embarrassing detail the story of her recent desertion by the man she loved. He had of course deserted her for some one else, and at the end of her remarkable narrative she sang, in a perfect debauch of emotion and self-pity: "But I am of a forgiving nature! Come back, come back, my rose, my heart, my soul—the bed is big enough for three!" Sometimes when there is a dance at a neighboring ranch the harpist and his son, who plays the jarana, stop at my place on their way home in the morning and play to me (the son also improvises) while I am at breakfast. The harpist is always drunk, and his instrument, after a night of hard work, out of tune. He appeared not long ago when I had staying with me a Boston lawyer—my only visitor so far this year.

"Isn't it horrible to eat soft boiled eggs and toast in this pandemonium," I called to him across the breakfast table.

"No," he answered, "it's splendid—it's just like being an Irish king."

D. H. LAWRENCE

(1885–1930)

D. H. Lawrence embarked on the voluntary exile he termed his "savage pilgrimage" after a period of controversy and persecution in England. His 1915 novel *The Rainbow* had been banned for obscenity, and during World War I he and his German-born wife, Frieda, were accused of spying for the Germans. Lawrence spent the rest of his life traveling in France, Italy, Sri Lanka (then Ceylon), Australia, the United States, and Mexico.

While he was suffering from tuberculosis, Lawrence and his wife lived in temperate Oaxaca. Though the novel he wrote in Mexico, *The Plumed Serpent* (1926), is not his best, the travel essays he published as *Mornings in Mexico* (1927) deftly and compassionately record the landscape, the villagers, and the cultural life of the place. The spectacle of market day extends back to pre-Columbian times and continues to this day as a riot of color, crafts, and produce that showcases the riches of rural Mexico.

From the valley villages and from the mountains the peasants and the Indians are coming in with supplies, the road is like a pilgrimage, with the dust in greatest haste, dashing for town. Dark-eared asses and running men, running women, running girls, running lads, twinkling donkeys ambling on fine little feet, under twin great baskets with tomatoes and gourds, twin great nets of bubble-shaped jars, twin bundles of neat-cut faggots of wood, neat as bunches of cigarettes, and twin net-sacks of charcoal. Donkeys, mules, on they come, great pannier baskets making a rhythm under the perched woman, great bundles bouncing against the sides of the slim-footed animals. A baby donkey trotting naked after its piled-up dam, a white, sandal-footed man following with the silent Indian haste, and a girl running again on light feet.

Onwards, on a strange current of haste. And slowly rowing among the foot-travel, the ox-wagons rolling solid wheels below the high net of the body. Slow oxen, with heads pressed down nosing to the earth, swaying, swaying their great horns as a snake sways itself, the shovel-shaped collar of solid wood pressing down on their necks like a scoop. On, on between the burnt-up turf and the solid, monumental green of the organ cactus. Past the rocks and the floating palo blanco flowers, past the towsled dust of the mesquite bushes. While the dust once more, in a greater haste than anyone, comes tall and rapid down the road, overpowering and obscuring all the little people, as in a cataclysm.

They are mostly small people, of the Zapotec race: small men with lifted chests and quick, lifted knees, advancing with heavy energy in the midst of dust. And quiet, small, round-headed women running barefoot, tightening their blue rebozos round their shoulders, so often with a baby in the fold. The white cotton clothes of the men so white that their faces are invisible places of darkness under their big hats. Clothed darkness, faces of night, quickly, silently, with inexhaustible energy advancing to the town.

And many of the Serranos, the Indians from the hills, wearing their little conical black felt hats, seem capped with night, above the straight white shoulders. Some have come far, walking all yesterday in their little black hats and black-sheathed sandals. To-morrow they will walk back. And their eyes will be just the same, black and bright and wild, in the dark faces. They have no goal, any more than the hawks in the air, and no course to run, any more than the clouds.

The market is a huge roofed-in place. Most extraordinary is the noise that comes out, as you pass along the adjacent street. It is a huge noise, yet you may never notice it. It sounds as if all the ghosts in the world were talking to one another, in ghost-voices, within the darkness of the market structure. It is a noise something like rain, or banana leaves in a wind. The market, full of Indians, dark-faced, silent-footed, hush-spoken, but pressing in in countless numbers. The queer hissing murmurs of the Zapotec *idioma*, among the sounds of Spanish, the quiet, aside-voices of the Mixtecas.

To buy and to sell, but above all, to commingle. In the old world, men make themselves two great excuses for coming together to a centre, and commingling freely in a mixed, unsuspicious host. Market and religion. These alone bring men, unarmed, together since time began. A little load of firewood, a woven blanket, a few eggs and tomatoes are excuse enough for men, women, and children to cross the foot-weary miles of valley and mountain. To buy, to sell, to barter, to exchange. To exchange, above all things, human contact.

That is why they like you to bargain, even if it's only the difference of a centavo. Round the centre of the covered market, where there is a basin of water, are the flowers: red, white, pink roses in heaps, many-coloured little carnations, poppies, bits of larkspur, lemon and orange marigolds, buds of madonna lilies, pansies, a few forget-me-nots. They don't bring the tropical flowers. Only the lilies come wild from the hills, and the mauve red orchids.

"How much this bunch of cherry-pie heliotrope?"

"Fifteen centavos."

"Ten."

"Fifteen."

You put back the cherry-pie, and depart. But the woman is quite content. The contact, so short even, brisked her up.

"Pinks?"

"The red ones, Señorita? Thirty centavos."

"No. I don't want red ones. The mixed."

"Ah!" The woman seizes a handful of little carnations of all colours, carefully puts them together. "Look, Señorita! No more?"

"No, no more. How much?"

"The same. Thirty centavos."

"It is much."

"No, Señorita, it is not much. Look at this little bunch. It is eight centavos."—Displays a scrappy little bunch. "Come then, twenty-five."

"No! Twenty-two."

"Look!" She gathers up three or four more flowers, and claps them to the bunch. "Two *reales*, Señorita."

It is a bargain. Off you go with multicoloured pinks, and the woman has had one more moment of contact, with a stranger, a perfect stranger. An intermingling of voices, a threading together of different wills. It is life. The centavos are an excuse.

The stalls go off in straight lines, to the right, brilliant vegetables, to the left, bread and sweet buns. Away at the one end, cheese, butter, eggs, chickens, turkeys, meat. At the other, the native-woven blankets and rebozos, skirts, shirts, handkerchiefs. Down the far-side, sandals and leather things.

The *sarape* men spy you, and whistle to you like ferocious birds, and call "Señor! Señor! Look!" Then with violence one flings open a dazzling blanket, while another whistles more ear-piercingly still, to make you look at *his* blanket. It is the veritable den of lions and tigers, that spot where the *sarape* men have their blankets piled on the ground. You shake your head, and flee.

To find yourself in the leather avenue.

"Señor! Señor! Look! Huaraches! Very fine, very finely made! Look Señor!"

The fat leather man jumps up and holds a pair of sandals at one's breast. They are of narrow woven strips of leather, in the newest Paris style, but a style ancient to these natives. You take them in your hand, and look at them quizzically, while the fat wife of the huarache man reiterates, "Very fine work. Very fine. Much work!"

Leather men usually seem to have their wives with them.

"How much?"

"Twenty *reales.*"

"Twenty!"—in a voice of surprise and pained indignation.

"How much do you give?"

You refuse to answer. Instead you put the huaraches to your nose. The huarache man looks at his wife, and they laugh aloud.

"They smell," you say.

"No, Señor, they don't smell!"—and the two go off into fits of laughter.

"Yes, they smell. It is not American leather."

"Yes, Señor, it is American leather. They don't smell, Señor. No, they don't smell." He coaxes you till you wouldn't believe your own nose.

"Yes, they smell."

"How much do you give?"

"Nothing, because they smell."

And you give another sniff, though it is painfully unnecessary. And in spite of your refusal to bid, the man and wife go into fits of laughter to see you painfully sniffing.

You lay down the sandals and shake your head.

"How much do you offer?" reiterates the man, gaily.

You shake your head mournfully, and move away. The leather man and his wife look at one another and go off into another fit of laughter, because you smelt the huaraches, and said they stank.

They did. The natives use human excrement for tanning leather. When Bernal Díaz came with Cortés to the great market-place of Mexico City, in Montezuma's day, he saw the little pots of human excrement in rows for sale, and the leather-makers going round sniffing to see which was the best, before they paid for it. It staggered even a fifteenth-century Spaniard. Yet my leather man and his wife think it screamingly funny that I smell the huaraches before buying them. Everything has its own smell, and the natural smell of huaraches is what it is. You might as well quarrel with an onion for smelling like an onion.

The great press of the quiet natives, some of them bright and clean, many in old rags, the brown flesh showing through the rents in the dirty cotton. Many wild hillmen, in their little hats of conical black felt, with their wild, staring eyes. And as they cluster round the hat-stall, in a long, long suspense of indecision before they can commit themselves, trying on a new hat, their black hair gleams blue-black, and falls thick and rich over their foreheads, like gleaming bluey-black feathers. And one is reminded again of the blue-haired Buddha, with the lotus at his navel.

But already the fleas are travelling under one's clothing.

Market lasts all day. The native inns are great dreary yards with little sheds, and little rooms around. Some men and families who have come from far, will sleep in one or other of the little stall-like rooms. Many will sleep on the stones, on the earth, round the market, anywhere. But the asses are there by the hundred, crowded in the inn-yards, drooping their ears with the eternal patience of the beast that knows better than any other beast that every road curves round to the same centre of rest, and hither and thither means nothing.

And towards nightfall the dusty road will be thronged with shadowy people and unladen asses and new-laden mules, urging silently into the country again, their backs to the town, glad to get away from the town, to see the cactus and the pleated hills, and the trees that mean a village. In some village they will lie under a tree, or under a wall, and sleep. Then the next day, home.

It is fulfilled, what they came to market for. They have sold and bought. But more than that, they have had their moment of contact and centripetal flow. They have been part of a great stream of men flowing to a centre, to the vortex of the market-place. And here they have felt life concentrate upon them, they have been jammed between the soft hot bodies of strange men come from afar, they have had the sound of strangers' voices in their ears, they have asked and been answered in unaccustomed ways.

There is no goal, and no abiding-place, and nothing is fixed, not even the cathedral towers. The cathedral towers are slowly leaning, seeking the curve of return. As the natives curved in a strong swirl, towards the vortex of the market. Then on a strong swerve of repulsion, curved out and away again, into space.

Nothing but the touch, the spark of contact. That, no more. That, which is most elusive, still the only treasure. Come, and gone, and yet the clue itself.

True, folded up in the handkerchief inside the shirt, are the copper centavos, and maybe a few silver pesos. But these too will disappear as the stars disappear at daybreak, as they are meant to disappear. Everything is meant to disappear. Every curve plunges into the vortex and is lost, re-emerges with a certain relief and takes to the open, and there is lost again.

Only that which is utterly intangible, matters. The contact, the spark of exchange. That which can never be fastened upon, forever gone, forever coming, never to be detained: the spark of contact.

Like the evening star, when it is neither night nor day. Like the evening star, between the sun and the moon, and swayed by neither of them. The flashing intermediary, the evening star that is seen only at the dividing of the day and night, but then is more wonderful than either.

DIANA KENNEDY

Often referred to as "the high priestess of Mexican cooking," Diana Kennedy was born and raised in England and first went to Mexico in 1957 with her husband, Paul Kennedy, a foreign correspondent for *The New York Times*. Fascinated with Mexican cuisine, she traveled the back roads and sampled regional cuisine from all over Mexico for over forty-five years. The result has been the publication of five cookbooks, including *My Mexico* (1998), *The Essential Cuisines of Mexico* (2000), and *From My Mexican Kitchen* (2003). She thoroughly debunks the idea of Mexican food as simple burritos and tacos, revealing it as the art form it truly is. From haute cuisine to street vendor food, the recipes she gathers illuminate the landscapes and cultures of Mexico.

Kennedy's book *My Mexico* not only contains recipes, but offers a travel account of the country, a personal retelling of the folklore and stories behind Mexican food. This excerpt on Campeche shows the way life revolves around traditional meals such as Sunday's *cochinita pibil*, a small pig seasoned with a paste of *achiote* and spices dissolved in bitter orange juice, wrapped in banana leaves, and cooked in a pit barbecue. The myriad herbs and spices listed have names that sound like neglected Mayan gods, such as *epazote* and *x-cat-ikes*. Kennedy marks the seasons by the ripening of fruits and bargains with fishermen for the local catch.

CAMPECHE

"Provincia azul, donde es azul el cielo, donde es azul el mar." "Blue region, where the sky is blue, where the sea is blue." I thought of this quote (from Carlos Pellicer) the other day as I was driving across the long bridge that links La Isla de Carmen to the mainland of Campeche. The sea and sky, both a pale lustrous blue, seem to converge at a hardly discernible line. There was nothing else to be seen but a few seabirds and an occasional fish jumping in the still water. I wondered if I dared stop on the bridge to take a photograph, but the trailers and trucks were coming up behind at a fast lick. When I come back, I thought.

On the journey back a storm had blown in and all was gray with silvery-green reflections of the mounting clouds in the water. Again it was impossible to stop as I watched the oncoming traffic in the rearview mirror—and besides, I would need a wide-angle lens to do justice to the beauty of that turbulent scene.

Campeche, the town, has always been a very special place for me. My first extended stay there to study the food was in the summer of 1969. The *Malecón* (promenade) stretched for several kilometers along the rim of the gulf, and the landfill between that and the town itself was dotted with a few buildings of hideous design and construction (I cannot use the word *architecture*). The *baluartes*, fortifications, built to defend the town against the most daring of pirates in the eighteenth century, stood back partially crumbling with neglect, the still elegant, whitish stone mottled with grays and blacks. Behind those walls lay the town itself; it was white and clean with immaculate small plazas overhung with flowering trees and shrubs surrounded by houses of simple but beautiful design that I have come to associate with that of the southern ports: Tlacotalpan, which is almost intact, and Veracruz, Alvarado, and Ciudad del Carmen, as they used to be.

In those days the market was small and compact, full of locally grown produce and fruits, and the eating stands served well-made regional specialties. I shall always remember the fish market. It stood on its own near the water's edge; it was light and cooled with breezes from the gulf. In the early morning fishermen brought their enormous catches of shrimp, shark, dogfish (*cazón*) of all sizes, and baskets of multicolored fish still squirming and shiny, fresh out of the water.

The outdoor cafés were always busy with local businessmen in white *guayaberas* passing the day gossiping and playing dominoes over numerous cups of coffee. Family life took place behind closed doors until the evening Mass, when the womenfolk sauntered through the *jardin* in front of the cathedral. And, of all the trivial things that I remember, there were no curtains at the bedroom windows of that ugly (and still ugly) hotel that faced the gulf. The lower half of the glass was only frosted and still not sufficiently opaque. As the sun dropped and the lights came on in the room, the local lads indulged in their favorite pastime of sitting on the promenade benches watching the unsuspecting visitors undress for bed or change to go out to supper.

When I visited some local cooks, mostly in restaurants, I noted over and over again through the years: "the freshest of fish, but grossly overcooked. Tasteless and watery." It was a little more difficult to ruin the solid-fleshed Morro crab claws, the specialty of Campeche at that time. (Some of those recipes are to be found in *The Cuisines of Mexico* and *Regional Mexican Cooking*.)

Ten years ago I happened to be driving back to Tabasco from Yucatán and stopped for the night in Campeche. I was dismayed; some of the lovely old houses had been replaced by modern monstrosities and the little plazas either destroyed or neglected. (I once again stayed at that ugly hotel, but this time the windows were curtained.) I stayed only through part of the morning and made this trivial observation in my notebook: "Is this the start of the

Campeche health movement? Stout matrons, hardly seen in the streets before, their hair still wrapped up in curlers, were walking in clutches in the early morning light, but nevertheless taking the opportunity of their newly acquired habit to catch up on the local gossip."

Recently I visited Campeche again, this time to stay longer and learn more about this very special place, not only from the point of view of its food but to see the countryside and the lesser-known (than those in Yucatán, for example) Mayan sites of Edzná, Calakmul, Chicanna, Becan, and Xpujil. Their magnificent tall structures, many with elaborate stone carvings, are awe-inspiring and especially impressive in their splendid isolation, surrounded as far as the eye can see by thickly wooded, untamed land.

By now the city had grown, spreading out over the surrounding hills, while the Malecón now extended even farther by landfill stretch along the water for many more kilometers. Today Campeche, ever noisy, is even more so, and the commercial streets bustle with life. The decay of the ramparts has been halted by a conservation order, which also includes the restoration of the elegant old homes and derelict buildings, bringing them back to a useful existence and restoring the architectural harmony of the past.

The *baluarte* of Santiago, for instance, has been transformed into a botanical garden for native plants, and the main thoroughfares have been planted with flowering trees. When I was there in May, the flame trees, *tabachín*, were ablaze with color alternating with the delicate *lluvia de oro* and their cascading bunches of yellow flowers and the pale pink *macuilis*.

At first glance the market seemed to have changed little; the small eateries were doing a brisk trade in the morning with *panuchos*, *pan de cazón*, and *negritos* (traditional specialties based on inflated tortillas stuffed with bean paste, etc. The freshly killed grass-fed beef still looked horribly red and tough (although, in fact, it has an excellent flavor), and you can still buy very large, fat white fowl for local dishes.

The fish market that used to be so colorful has been incorporated into the main market building and isn't as picturesque as it used to be. Most of the fishermen now sell their catch where their boats come in and are moored, on the malecón. All complain that stocks of fish are diminishing. Undoubtedly overfishing, illegal catching in the closed seasons, and the natural foods of the fish being destroyed by contamination of the waters nearer the shore all play their part. However, most of the blame belongs to the government-owned petroleum industry, Pemex, which has flagrantly disregarded the preventive measures against polluting the sea while giving lip service to them.

One long counter in the market is devoted to *cazón asado*, grilled dogfish, sold alongside the herbs and condiments with which it is cooked: flat-leaf parsley, chives, *epazote*, *chiles habaneros*, and *güeros*, called here *x-cat-ik*.

Outside the main market building is a covered area where mountains of fresh chiles are sold, all colors at all stages of ripeness: habaneros, *dulces*, *verdes*, *rosados*, *x-cat-ikes*. There are *chaya* leaves, dark green squash formed like pattypan, and fresh *ibes*— light green flecked with black, shucked then and there from their long, skinny, green pods.

At last I was here in May for the *marañon* season—the brilliantly colored fruits of the cashew nut. The sidewalks around the market were perfumed by these exotic fruits, smelling and tasting like strong, very ripe strawberries. A few days earlier I had seen them growing, hanging down from the trees like small, shiny red lanterns terminating with that curious formation resembling a parrot's beak in a shiny gray casing, the cashew nut. Some of the fruits were a deep salmon-pink color, and others, from a different tree, were yellow. For the whole of my stay, *agua de marañon* (*Ana-*

cardium occidentale) was served with every midday meal. One of the traditional cooks told me that on no account must the flesh of the fruit be put into the blender; it had to be mashed by hand. I can vouch for it that this is the best method. It is the most exotically perfumed drink of any I know.

The home cooks that I visited and cooked with still prepare daily their traditional recipes and take great pride in them; it is their "soul food." Strong Mayan influences can be seen in the preparation and ingredients of many of the local dishes, while others show a complete melding of Mayan and Spanish, and still others have a distinctive Lebanese influence—there are large Lebanese communities of long standing in the Yucatecan peninsula.

For those families who still follow traditional eating patterns, there is a predictable weekly sequence to the dishes prepared: on Mondays it is *comida de floja* (the lazy woman's meal—although it still requires a lot of preparation), *frijol con puerco*, beans and pork (recipe in *Regional Mexican Cooking*). On Tuesdays beef is served in some form or other, often thin steaks in a tomato sauce, breaded, or stewed with charred onion and garlic, seasoned with oregano, and served with plain white rice. To digress: I am very partial to the rice grown in this state—it has a very satisfying, earthy flavor that reminds me of the rice from Guayana that I remember eating years ago on the Caribbean Islands. Sadly, as with many other good things, production is dwindling because of the low prices paid to the producers.

Wednesday is the day for preparing a simple *puchero*, or stew, with chicken or beef with vegetables, and Thursday for *cazón* (dogfish) in any one of its various preparations. On Friday my friends and their cooks like to choose a whole fish, or fish steaks, often seasoned with tomato and *chile dulce* and cooked in a banana leaf.

Every Saturday cattle are slaughtered to ensure an abundance of beef for the Sunday *puchero de tres carnes* (stew of three meats).

The fresh offal is immediately bought up for *chocolomo*, a hearty soup/stew served only on Saturdays.

In spite of the hot climate freshened somewhat by breezes from the sea, Sunday is a day of heavy eating. In the early morning there was a steady stream of people going to their favorite cook, usually a man, of *cochinita pibil.* A small, but not suckling, pig is seasoned with a paste of *achiote* and spices dissolved in bitter orange juice, wrapped in banana leaves, and cooked in a pit barbecue. The stomach and large intestines are stuffed and cooked with the meat. A slice of this *buche* and the roughly shredded pork is stuffed into the Campeche-style French bread roll, for breakfast.

The main meal of the day is a *puchero de las tres carnes*, the most substantial of stews with pork, beef, and a fat hen (the hen is very important for flavor). The meat is served with the vegetables, a bowl of the broth on the side along with a helping of rice and the typical relishes of the region: chopped onion in Seville orange juice, a *salpicón*, radishes chopped with cilantro and chile, again in orange juice, and (another relish) *chile habanero* charred and crushed. Now, I like my food piping hot, so I never know where to start first; picking at this and that at random, I am full far too early in the game, to my annoyance. A Sunday *puchero* is an excellent prelude to a long siesta. If there is meat left over, it is shredded and added to mashed vegetables for tacos.

Eating patterns are always more likely to change in the larger urban centers, while in the more isolated rural areas there has to be much more reliance on ingredients readily available. One family I know that lives in Campeche, but also has a ranch about ninety kilometers away, remembers being brought up on what it cultivated: corn, beans, squash, roots, vegetables in various guises, and wild game, especially venison—before the shooting of it was forbidden to conserve rapidly dwindling stocks.

Sra. Concepción told me about the preparation of the ritual food for the *comida de milpa* (food of the cornfield), *El han-li-cool,* which she still prepares under the guidance of her father, who was a strong believer that the gods of the mountain have to be appeased to ensure a good harvest, to pray for rain, or to give thanks for a good harvest. She remembers as a young woman how the corn flourished in the field where the offering was made, while other fields that had been planted were not nearly so lush and pro-ductive.

After the ritual killing of turkeys and chickens with prayers chanted in Mayan, the food was cooked in a pit in the ground, *pib*, dug in the field to be blessed. There was *pan de milpa* or *gordas*, nine or thirteen layers of corn *masa* between alternate layers of pureed beans and toasted ground pumpkin seeds, the whole wrapped in banana leaves. When the meal was served, part of it was crumbled into the broth from the meats. There were also *bolillitos*, indeed like small, round *bolillos* (bobbin-shaped bread rolls), also filled. These are eaten together with the fat skimmed off the meat broth.

Without doubt, one of the most important foods in Campeche is *cazón* or dogfish. There are at least five species: *cagüay*, *t'uc t'un*, *cornua*, *pech*, and *jaquetón*. These are much preferred over shark, a near relative, for having firmer and less watery meat. Of course, everyone has a preference and will argue hotly in favor of one or the other. Another strong preference is between fresh *cazón* and *asado*, the latter grilled until it is slightly charred. The *cazón asado* in the market was not prepared by the vendors but principally by one man. I thought it would be interesting to see just how it was pre-pared and, directed by neighbors, went to see him. No, he made all sorts of excuses, including the fact that he did the grilling at four in the morning. Nobody believed him. Perhaps he thought I would set up in competition until someone pointed out that I did arrive in a black police car (lent by a friend in the Justice Depart-ment) with a burly escort/chauffeur—that was enough to make anyone suspicious.

TOM MILLER

(1 9 4 7 –)

Tom Miller has been writing about the American Southwest and Latin America for more than three decades. His nine books take readers to the Andes, the Caribbean, Mexico, and the U.S. borderlands. In his book *Jack Ruby's Kitchen Sink* (2000), Miller explores from the American Southwest to the Gulf of Mexico, chronicling some of the livelier—and seamier—aspects of the region, from cockfighting and illegal border crossings to battles with saguaro cactus. The book won the prestigious Lowell Thomas Award for Best Travel Book of the Year in 2001.

This excerpt is from the essay "Searching for the Heart of La Bamba," in which the author travels to Veracruz and traces the origins of the song "La Bamba." Miller has amassed some eighty versions of "La Bamba"—among them one from Israel, another with Andean flutes, and a third by a Tohono O'odham band. He writes, "As obsessions go, collecting 'La Bamba' has all the elements of harmless passion: boundless exuberance, unrestrained elasticity, and endless variations. I reduced my studies of bambalogy to ten versions so they'd fit on a record." This record, *The Best of La Bamba* (1988), concludes with the majestic jarocho ditty sung by the Mormon Tabernacle Choir.

The song "La Bamba" began its cross-cultural odyssey in Veracruz, on Mexico's Gulf Coast, where, wrote Carlos Fuentes about his ancestral home state, "the extraordinary local bands, based on the harp and the guitar, beat a lovely sensuous rhythm throughout the night." He was writing of *jarocho* music, a style that fuses European, African, and Caribbean qualities. It is characterized by the playfulness of its lyrics and its stringed instruments—guitars in various sizes, a small harp, often a stand-up bass, and sometimes a violin. Ever since Hernán Cortés landed on the Gulf Coast in 1519, Veracruz has seen the arrival of Catholic missionaries, Caribbean pirates, African slaves, foreign troops, and seafaring traders. The result was a fusion of Spanish tradition with African, Caribbean, and native life. This mixed-blood population came to be called mestizo, and its songs, coupled with unique dances and rhythms, were known in Veracruz as jarocho-style songs. Of the hundreds and hundreds of tunes that evolved from that hybrid, "La Bamba" is the most durable.

Although its popularity is assured, "La Bamba's" origins are still unknown. The Spanish brought slaves to the Gulf Coast in the early 1600s from six parts of western Africa, including a place called Mbamba. Could "La Bamba" have been a blend of Spanish and an African tongue? Probably so, says *Sones de la tierra*, a book on Veracruz music: "The name Bamba evokes the original province of the black Congolese." A number of West African tribes, rivers, and towns are named using various forms of the word "bamba." In Veracruz the song gained local notoriety not long after a pirate named Lorencillo attacked the town in 1683, an event sung about in a late 1600s' version of "La Bamba."

As veracruzano minstrels and troubadours traveled out of the region and from one Mexican town to another, "La Bamba" spread, infecting the countryside with its rhythms and song. One historian places the first recorded version of "La Bamba" in 1908. In the following decades, 250,000-watt clear-channel radio station XEW broadcast the song and other standards from Mexico City to pueblos throughout the country and beyond. It became a favorite in Garibaldi Plaza, Mexico City, which has been a musicians' gathering place since the 1920s. Starting in the late 1930s, Mexico's burgeoning film industry exploited the country's regional folk styles, often with a nightclub-cum-brothel dance scene, and Mexican composers celebrating regional traditions have woven the song into symphonic scores. By World War II, "La Bamba" had reached into every home, every cabaret and concert hall, and every movie theater in the republic.

"La Bamba" gained its widest popularity when Miguel Alemán, a Veracruz native, became Mexico's president in 1946. It was during the Alemán years that northbound migrant labor carried the song into the American border states. Wherever Alemán was received in the world, welcoming bands would strike up "La Bamba." Tropical music was in its heyday and the instantly recognizable "La Bamba" quickly became a favorite at newly opened nightclubs in Acapulco and Tijuana. The wife of the American ambassador to Mexico, said the press, had danced to "La Bamba" at a state affair, much to the chagrin of veracruzanos, who saw their rustic ditty being taken over by high society. It became Mexico's signature song.

Mexico is a country whose capital dominates the national culture, and jarocho music has found its niche there, preserved to a healthy degree by the musicians from Veracruz who weave among Mexico City's pedestrians and diners. I met Raúl Rosas Santos at El Chimbombo, where he played daily, and we drove over to his house near the airport to talk. Rosas, who came to Mexico City many years back "to play the tables," had a reputation for inventing songs on the spur of the moment.

"I am a decrepit old man," said Rosas, who appeared neither worn nor aged. "It gives me great pleasure to tell you about our folklore. I'm lacking a bit in culture, but people love our music. We make up verses on the spur of the moment, depending on what's happening, and we make it rhyme. Sometimes we tell jokes with double entendre and eroticism. We speak of politics and international events. We're like local reporters, only we do it in verse form.

"The evolution of 'La Bamba' is like an invention of Thomas Edison's—first it's rudimentary, then you begin adding things.

That song has been very popular wherever I've played." Without warning, Rosas pulled out his guitar and composed a jarocho song about my visit to his home. More up to date than that he could not get.

My passion for "La Bamba" has also carried me to Veracruz. Although modern inconveniences have reduced the city's tranquillity that Carlos Fuentes wrote of, the appeal of its white architecture, its warm sea breezes, and its inhabitants' gentility still set it apart from Mexico's more cosmopolitan centers. I learned during my first visits there in the 1980s that mornings are best begun at Café de la Parroquia, next to the Zócalo. The café's origins date back to the early 1800s, by which time "La Bamba" had already traveled throughout Mexico.

Despite the early hour, jarocho music is never far from veracruzano ears. Two men dressed in white walked by carrying a long marimba, then plopped it down and started playing. Believing that no day in Veracruz should begin without "La Bamba," I asked them to play the song. The delicacy of its rhythm and tone startled me; they played to the tempo of a fluttering butterfly. When the marimberos had finished "La Bamba," they proffered a small notepad listing a hundred more songs in their repertoire. I declined to choose one and paid them their three dollars. They picked up their marimba and strolled over to the next café. The nighttime sensuality that Carlos Fuentes rhapsodized about enveloped the morning as well.

Xalapa, Veracruz's capital, lay inland, two hours northwest, more than 4,000 feet above sea level. It's a university town known for its orchestra and music department, and it is filled with art galleries, coffeehouses, bookstores, and nightclubs. When I stepped off the bus, the opening lyrics to "La Bamba" greeted me: *Para bailar la bamba, se necesita una poca de gracia*—To dance la bamba, you need a little bit of grace. And elegance was in fact evident in Xalapa, especially in the persons of Sara Arróñez Ramírez, a dance instructor, and Manolo, her partner. As the song played on a cassette I carried with me, the two demonstrated the dance.

With the opening notes, Manolo's sash was unwrapped from his waist and laid on the ground. In rhythm, the two moved up and back on either side of it. Then, with her left foot, Sara reshaped the sash into something resembling a backward *S*. Using their feet, lifting and tugging, pulling and holding, the couple maneuvered the sash into a neatly tied bow. Manolo lifted it with his foot, grabbed one loop with one hand, and placed the other loop around Sara.

"It's easy once you get the hang of it," Sara said afterward at a nearby café, "but fewer and fewer people know how to do it."

"You know," I said in passing, "there was a very popular rock-and-roll version of 'La Bamba' in the United States."

"*¡No!*" she cried, as she put a hand to her face. "*¡No me diga!*" Say it ain't so!

Sara would have been less horrified by the changing lyrics to the song, as new words have been a hallmark of Veracruz music since jarocho culture emerged from the African, Spanish, and native cultural ménage à trois. At the height of the Chicano movement in the 1970s, activists sang a version called "La Bamba Chicana," with the line *Para ser Chicano, se necesita un poquito de boicot*—To be Chicano requires a little bit of boycott. Another version changes "bamba" to "bomba" and becomes an anti-nuclear-bomb rendition. In the 1700s, Roman Catholic priests in Veracruz frowned on songs such as "La Bamba," which encouraged suggestive body movements and double entendre, yet today the sanctity and solemnity of religious music embraces that same song. Nowhere is this more evident than in "La Bamba" sung by the Mormon Tabernacle Choir.

REVOLUTIONARY ENCOUNTERS

¡Que Viva Mexico!

ARCHIBALD MACLEISH

(1892–1982)

Archibald MacLeish, who served as editor at *Fortune* magazine and as assistant secretary of state for cultural affairs, received the Pulitzer Prize three times: for his play *J.B.* in 1958, his *Collected Poems* in 1952, and, the first time, for his epic poem *Conquistador* in 1932.

In order to research this poem, MacLeish went to Mexico in 1928 and retraced the journey of Cortés's army through Mexico. The poem is written from the point of view of Bernal Díaz, who accompanied Cortés, and it alternately grapples with the fate of the common soldier in a foreign land and the morality of the conquest of the Aztecs. In this excerpt, the Aztec woman La Malinche, or Doña Marína as she is called by the Spaniards, is present, translating for Cortés and his men. She is one of Mexico's most intriguing historical figures—the translator and lover of Cortés who gave birth to the first *mestizo* in Mexico. In Octavio Paz's book, *The Labyrinth of Solitude,* he refers to her as "The Mexican Eve."

And the girl Marína spoke it to Aguilár:
And Aguilár interpreted—'Montezúma
'Emperor over the earth and of those stars:

'The sun is toward him and the altering moon:
'He has beheld your shadows in his houses:
'His are the lands: the glass of the sea knew you:

'Now does he send you from his endless thousands
'These and this treasure: in Tenochtitlán
'Armies are harvested like summer's flowers:'

So did he speak and he pointed with raised hand
Westward out of the sun: and Cortés was silent
And he looked long at his feet at the furrowed sand:

And his voice when he spoke was a grave voice without guile
     in it—
'Say that we thank him well: say also
'We would behold this Emperor:' and he smiled:

And the voice of Marína cried in the sea fall
And they stood on the dunes and were still and the sky back of
     them:
And their plumes moved in the wind as the tree tosses:

And he that had spoken—'Proud and ignorant man!
'Hardly now is your heel's mark on these grasses:
'The grooves of your ships go down to the sea bank:

'Already you name that king! West of the passes:
'Westward of Xícho and of Ixuacán
'And the salt plains and the corn plains and the pastures:

'West of the city where the earth-mound stands:
'West of the burning and the woman mountain:
'There is his town: there is Tenochtitlán:

'The clean wave runs among the island flowers:
'Ancient is all that earth: a long-used dwelling:
'The dead are silent in that ashy ground:

'Old are the gods there:—in the stone-made shelters
'Utter the dry bones their unspoken names:
'The locusts answer in the summer nettles:

'None have conquered that land . . .'

                                          and they: as they came to us . . .

JOHN REED

(1887–1920)

John Reed was born in Portland, Oregon, into a wealthy family, attended Harvard, and then worked as a journalist for leftist magazines. He's best known for his book *Ten Days That Shook the World* (1918), about the Bolshevik Revolution in Russia. In 1914 Reed went to Mexico to cover the Mexican Revolution for *Metropolitan Magazine* and *New York World*. He spent four months with Pancho Villa and his troops and described the revolutionary fighting in *Insurgent Mexico* (1914), a collection of stories about the characters and battles of the Mexican Revolution that he published himself.

In 1911, with the cry of "Land and Liberty," Emiliano Zapata led an uprising in the southern state of Morelos, calling for agrarian reform. In 1913, General Huerta turned against the newly elected President Madero, forced him to resign, and ordered that he be executed. After Madero's death, the armed struggle began in earnest. Francisco "Pancho" Villa returned from exile in El Paso, organized the Northern Division, and began leading troops and taking over northern Mexico. Reed traveled with the fighters during this time, embedding with them during some of the fiercest battles and drinking and dancing with them during the pauses. Reed found humor and irony in the wartime bravado he witnessed. His book, which has since been reprinted many times, is an engaging account not only of the leaders of Mexico's revolution, but also of the ordinary people.

THE RISE OF A BANDIT

Villa was an outlaw for twenty-two years. When he was only a boy of sixteen, delivering milk in the streets of Chihuahua, he killed a government official and had to take to the mountains. The story is that the official had violated his sister, but it seems probable that Villa killed him on account of his insufferable insolence. That in itself would not have outlawed him long in Mexico, where human life is cheap; but once a refugee he committed the unpardonable crime of stealing cattle from the rich *hacendados*. And from that time to the outbreak of the Madero revolution the Mexican government had a price on his head.

Villa was the son of ignorant peons. He had never been to school. He hadn't the slightest conception of the complexity of civilization, and when he finally came back to it, a mature man of extraordinary native shrewdness, he encountered the twentieth century with the naïve simplicity of a savage.

It is almost impossible to procure accurate information about his career as a bandit. There are accounts of outrages he committed in old files of local newspapers and government reports, but those sources are prejudiced, and his name became so prominent as a bandit that every train robbery and holdup and murder in northern Mexico was attributed to Villa. But an immense body of popular legend grew up among the peons around his name. There are many traditional songs and ballads celebrating his exploits— you can hear the shepherds singing them around their fires in the mountains at night, repeating verses handed down by their fathers or composing others extemporaneously. For instance, they tell the story of how Villa, fired by the story of the misery of the peons on the Hacienda of Los Alamos, gathered a small army and descended upon the Big House, which he looted, and distributed the spoils among the poor people. He drove off thousands of cattle from the Terrazzas range and ran them across the border. He would suddenly descend upon a prosperous mine and seize the bullion. When he needed corn he captured a granary belonging to some rich man. He recruited almost openly in the villages far removed from the well-traveled roads and railways, organizing the outlaws of the mountains. Many of the present rebel soldiers used to belong to his band and several of the Constitutionalist generals, like Urbina. His range was confined mostly to southern Chihuahua and northern Durango, but it extended from Coahuila right across the Republic to the State of Sinaloa.

His reckless and romantic bravery is the subject of countless poems. They tell, for example, how one of his band named Reza was captured by the *rurales* and bribed to betray Villa. Villa heard of it and sent word into the city of Chihuahua that he was coming for Reza. In broad daylight he entered the city on horseback, took ice cream on the Plaza—the ballad is very explicit on this point— and rode up and down the streets until he found Reza strolling with his sweetheart in the Sunday crowd on the Paseo Bolivar, where he shot him and escaped. In time of famine he fed whole districts, and took care of entire villages evicted by the soldiers under Porfirio Díaz's outrageous land law. Everywhere he was known as The Friend of the Poor. He was the Mexican Robin Hood.

In all these years he learned to trust nobody. Often in his secret journeys across the country with one faithful companion he camped in some desolate spot and dismissed his guide; then, leaving a fire burning, he rode all night to get away from the faithful companion. That is how Villa learned the art of war, and in the field today, when the army comes into camp at night, Villa flings the bridle of his horse to an orderly, takes a serape over his shoulder, and sets out for the hills alone. He never seems to sleep. In the dead of night he will appear somewhere along the line of outposts to see if the sentries are on the job; and in the morning he returns from a totally different direction. No one, not even the most trusted officer of his staff, knows the last of his plans until he is ready for action.

When Madero took the field in 1910, Villa was still an outlaw. Perhaps, as his enemies say, he saw a chance to whitewash himself; perhaps, as seems probable, he was inspired by the Revolution of the peons. Anyway, about three months after they rose in arms, Villa suddenly appeared in El Paso and put himself, his band, his knowledge of the country, and all his fortune at the command of Madero. The vast wealth that people said he must have accumulated during his twenty years of robbery turned out to be 363 silver *pesos*, badly worn. Villa became a Captain in the Maderista army, and as such went to Mexico City with Madero and was made honorary general of the new *rurales*. He was attached to Huerta's army when it was sent north to put down the Orozco Revolution. Villa commanded the garrison of Parral, and defeated Orozco with an inferior force in the only decisive battle of the war.

Huerta put Villa in command of the advance, and let him and the veterans of Madero's army do the dangerous and dirty work while the old line Federal regiments lay back under the protection of their artillery. In Jimenez Huerta suddenly summoned Villa before a court-martial and charged him with insubordination—claiming to have wired an order to Villa in Parral, which order Villa said he never received. The court-martial lasted fifteen minutes, and Huerta's most powerful future antagonist was sentenced to be shot.

Alfonso Madero, who was on Huerta's staff, stayed the execution, but President Madero, forced to back up the orders of his commander in the field, imprisoned Villa in the penitentiary of the capital. During all this time Villa never wavered in his loyalty to Madero—an unheard-of thing in Mexican history. For a long time he had passionately wanted an education. Now he wasted no time in regrets or political intrigue. He set himself with all his force to learn to read and write. Villa hadn't the slightest foundation to work upon. He spoke the crude Spanish of the very poor—what is called *pelado*. He knew nothing of the rudiments or philosophy of language; and he started out to learn those first, because he always must know the *why* of things. In nine months he could write a very fair hand and read the newspapers. It is interesting now to see him read, or, rather, hear him, for he has to drone the words aloud like a small child. Finally, the Madero government connived at his escape from prison, either to save Huerta's face because Villa's friends had demanded an investigation, or because Madero was convinced of his innocence and didn't dare openly to release him.

From that time to the outbreak of the last revolution, Villa lived in El Paso, Texas, and it was from there that he set out, in April, 1913, to conquer Mexico with four companions, three led horses, two pounds of sugar and coffee, and a pound of salt.

There is a little story connected with that. He hadn't money enough to buy horses, nor had any of his companions. But he sent two of them to a local livery stable to rent riding horses every day for a week. They always paid carefully at the end of the ride, so when they asked for eight horses the livery stable man had no hesitation about trusting them with them. Six months later, when Villa came triumphantly into Juarez at the head of an army of four thousand men, the first public act he committed was to send a man with double the price of the horses to the owner of the livery stable.

He recruited in the mountains near San Andres, and so great was his popularity that within one month he had raised an army of three thousand men; in two months he had driven the Federal garrisons all over the State of Chihuahua back into Chihuahua City;

in six months he had taken Torreon; and in seven and a half Juarez had fallen to him, Mercado's Federal army had evacuated Chihuahua, and northern Mexico was almost free.

THE HUMAN SIDE

Villa has two wives, one a patient, simple woman who was with him during all his years of outlawry, who lives in El Paso, and the other a cat-like, slender young girl, who is the mistress of his house in Chihuahua. He is perfectly open about it, though lately the educated, conventional Mexicans who have been gathering about him in ever-increasing numbers have tried to hush up the fact. Among the peons it is not only not unusual but customary to have more than one mate.

One hears a great many stories of Villa's violating women. I asked him if that were true. He pulled his mustache and stared at me for a minute with an inscrutable expression. "I never take the trouble to deny such stories," he said. "They say I am a bandit, too. Well, you know my history. But tell me; have you ever met a husband, father, or brother of any woman that I have violated?" He paused: "Or even a witness?"

It is fascinating to watch him discover new ideas. Remember that he is absolutely ignorant of the troubles and confusions and readjustments of modern civilization. "Socialism," he said once, when I wanted to know what he thought of it: "Socialism—is it a thing? I only see it in books, and I do not read much." Once I asked him if women would vote in the new Republic. He was sprawled out on his bed, with his coat unbuttoned. "Why, I don't think so," he said, startled, suddenly sitting up. "What do you mean—vote? Do you mean elect a government and make laws?" I said I did and that women already were doing it in the United States. "Well," he said, scratching his head, "if they do it up there I don't see that they shouldn't do it down here." The idea seemed to amuse him enormously. He rolled it over and over in his mind, looking at me and away again. "It may be as you say," he said, "but I have never thought about it. Women seem to me to be things to protect, to love. They have no sternness of mind. They can't consider anything for its right or wrong. They are full of pity and softness. Why," he said, "a woman would not give an order to execute a traitor."

"I am not so sure of that, *mi General*," I said. "Women can be crueller and harder than men."

He stared at me, pulling his mustache. And then he began to grin. He looked slowly to where his wife was setting the table for lunch. "*Oiga*," he said, "come here. Listen. Last night I caught three traitors crossing the river to blow up the railroad. What shall I do with them? Shall I shoot them or not?"

Embarrassed, she seized his hand and kissed it. "Oh, I don't know anything about that," she said. "You know best."

"No," said Villa. "I leave it entirely to you. Those men were going to try to cut our communications between Juarez and Chihuahua. They were traitors—Federals. What shall I do? Shall I shoot them or not?"

"Oh, well, shoot them," said Mrs. Villa.

Villa chuckled delightedly. "There is something in what you say," he remarked, and for days afterward went around asking the cook and the chambermaids whom they would like to have for President of Mexico.

He never missed a bullfight, and every afternoon at four o'clock he was to be found at the cockpit, where he fought his own birds with the happy enthusiasm of a small boy. In the evening he played faro in some gambling hall. Sometimes in the late morning he would send a fast courier after Luis Leon, the bullfighter, and telephone personally to the slaughterhouse, asking if they had any fierce bulls in the pen. They almost always did have, and we would all get on horseback and gallop through the streets about a mile to the big adobe corrals. Twenty cowboys cut the bull out of the herd, threw and tied him and cut off his sharp horns, and then Villa and Luis Leon and anybody else who wanted to would take the professional red capes and go down into the ring; Luis Leon with professional caution, Villa as stubborn and clumsy as the bull, slow on his feet, but swift as an animal with his body and arms. Villa would walk right up to the pawing, infuriated animal, and, with his double cape, slap him insolently across the face, and, for half an hour, would follow the greatest sport I ever saw. Sometimes the sawed-off horns of the bull would catch Villa in the seat of the trousers and propel him violently across the ring; then he would turn and grab the bull by the head and wrestle with him with the sweat streaming down his face until five or six *compañeros* seized the bull's tail and hauled him plowing and bellowing back.

Villa never drinks nor smokes, but he will outdance the most ardent *novio* in Mexico. When the order was given for the army to advance upon Torreon, Villa stopped off at the Camargo to be best man at the wedding of one of his old *compadres*. He danced steadily without stopping, they said, all Monday night, all Tuesday, and all Tuesday night, arriving at the front on Wednesday morning with bloodshot eyes and an air of extreme lassitude.

"ON TO TORREON!"

At Yermo there is nothing but leagues and leagues of sandy desert, sparsely covered with scrubby mesquite and dwarf cactus, stretching away on the west to jagged, tawny mountains, and on the east to a quivering skyline of plain. A battered water tank, with too little dirty alkali water, a demolished railway station shot to pieces by Orozco's cannon two years before, and a switch track compose the town. There is no water to speak of for forty miles. There is no grass for animals. For three months in the spring bitter, parching winds drive the yellow dust across it.

Along the single track in the middle of the desert lay ten enormous trains, pillars of fire by night and of black smoke by day,
stretching back northward farther than the eye could reach.
Around them, in the chaparral, camped nine thousand men without shelter, each man's horse tied to the mesquite beside him,
where hung his one serape and red strips of drying meat. From
fifty cars horses and mules were being unloaded. Covered with
sweat and dust, a ragged trooper plunged into a cattle car among
the flying hoofs, swung himself upon a horse's back, and jabbed
his spurs deep in, with a yell. Then came a terrific drumming of
frightened animals, and suddenly a horse shot violently from the
open door, usually backward, and the car belched flying masses of
horses and mules. Picking themselves up, they fled in terror,
snorting through wide nostrils at the smell of the open. Then the
wide, watchful circle of troopers turned *vaqueros* lifted the great
coils of their lassoes through the choking dust, and the running
animals swirled round and round upon one another in a panic.
Officers, orderlies, generals with their staffs, soldiers with halters,
hunting for their mounts, galloped and ran past in inextricable
confusion. Bucking mules were being harnessed to the caissons.
Troopers who had arrived on the last trains wandered about looking for their brigades. Way ahead some men were shooting at a
rabbit. From the tops of the boxcars and the flatcars, where they
were camped by hundreds, the *soldaderas* and their half-naked
swarms of children looked down, screaming shrill advice and
asking everybody in general if they had happened to see Juan
Moñeros, or Jesus Hernandez, or whatever the name of their
man happened to be. . . . One man trailing a rifle wandered along
shouting that he had had nothing to eat for two days and he
couldn't find his woman who made his *tortillas* for him, and
he opined that she had deserted him to go with some ——— of
another brigade. . . . The women on the roofs of the cars said,

"Valgame Dios!" and shrugged their shoulders; then they dropped
him down some three-days-old *tortillas*, and asked him, for the love
he bore Our Lady of Guadalupe, to lend them a cigarette. A clamorous, dirty throng stormed the engine of our train, screaming for
water. When the engineer stood them off with a revolver, telling
them there was plenty of water in the water train, they broke away
and aimlessly scattered, while a fresh throng took their places.
Around the twelve immense tank cars, a fighting mass of men and
animals struggled for a place at the little faucets ceaselessly pouring. Above the place a mighty cloud of dust, seven miles long and
a mile wide, towered up into the still, hot air, and, with the black
smoke of the engines, struck wonder and terror into the Federal
outposts fifty miles away on the mountains back of Mapimi.

When Villa left Chihuahua for Torreon, he closed the telegraph
wires to the north, stopped train service to Juarez, and forbade on
pain of death that anyone should carry or send news of his departure to the United States. His object was to take the Federals by
surprise, and it worked beautifully. No one, not even Villa's staff,
knew when he would leave Chihuahua; the army had delayed there
so long that we all believed it would delay another two weeks. And
then Saturday morning we woke to find the telegraph and railway
cut, and three huge trains, carrying the Brigada Gonzales-Ortega,
already gone. The Zaragosa left the next day, and Villa's own
troops the following morning. Moving with the swiftness that
always characterizes him, Villa had his entire army concentrated at
Yermo the day afterward, without the Federals knowing that he
had left Chihuahua.

There was a mob around the portable field telegraph that had
been rigged up in the ruined station. Inside, the instrument was
clicking. Soldiers and officers indiscriminately choked up the windows and the door, and every once in a while the operator would
shout something in Spanish and a perfect roar of laughter would

go up. It seemed that the telegraph had accidentally tapped a wire that had not been destroyed by the Federals—a wire that connected with the Federal military wire from Mapimi to Torreon.

"Listen!" cried the operator. "Colonel Argumedo in command of the *cabecillos colorados* in Mapimi is telegraphing to General Velasco in Torreon. He says that he sees smoke and a big dust cloud to the north, and thinks that some rebel troops are moving south from Escalon!"

Night came, with a cloudy sky and a rising wind that began to lift the dust. Along the miles and miles of trains, the fires of the *soldaderas* flared from the tops of the freight cars. Out into the desert so far that finally they were mere pinpoints of flame stretched the innumerable campfires of the army, half obscured by the thick, billowing dust. The storm completely concealed us from Federal watchers. "Even God," remarked Major Leyva, "even God is on the side of Francisco Villa!" We sat at dinner in our converted boxcar, with young, great-limbed, expressionless General Maximo García and his brother, the even huger red-faced Benito García, and little Major Manuel Acosta, with the beautiful manners of his race. García had long been holding the advance at Escalon. He and his brothers—one of whom, José García, the idol of the army, had been killed in battle but a short four years ago—were wealthy *hacendados*, owners of immense tracts of land. They had come out with Madero. . . . I remember that he brought us a jug of whisky, and refused to discuss the Revolution, declaring that he was fighting for better whisky! As I write this comes a report that he is dead from a bullet wound received in the battle of Sacramento. . . .

Out in the dust storm, on a flatcar immediately ahead of ours, some soldiers lay around their fire with their heads in their women's laps, singing "The Cockroach," which tells in hundreds of satirical verses what the Constitutionalists would do when they captured Juarez and Chihuahua from Mercado and Orozco.

Above the wind one was aware of the immense sullen murmur of the host, and occasionally some sentry challenged in a falsetto howl: *"Quien vive?"* And the answer: *"Chiapas!" "Que gente?" "Chao!"* . . . Through the night sounded the eerie whistle of the ten locomotives at intervals as they signaled back and forth to one another.

THE ARMY AT YERMO

At dawn next morning General Toribio Ortega came to the car for breakfast—a lean, dark Mexican, who is called "The Honorable" and "The Most Brave" by the soldiers. He is by far the most simple-hearted and disinterested soldier in Mexico. He never kills his prisoners. He has refused to take a cent from the Revolution beyond his meager salary. Villa respects and trusts him perhaps beyond all his Generals. Ortega was a poor man, a cowboy. He sat there, with his elbows on the table, forgetting his breakfast, his big eyes flashing, smiling his gentle, crooked smile, and told us why he was fighting.

"I am not an educated man," he said. "But I know that to fight is the last thing for any people. Only when things get too bad to stand, eh? And, if we are going to kill our brothers, something fine must come out of it, eh? You in the United States do not know what we have seen, we Mexicans! We have looked on at the robbing of our people, the simple, poor people, for thirty-five years, eh? We have seen the *rurales* and the soldiers of Porfirio Díaz shoot down our brothers and our fathers, and justice denied to them. We have seen our little fields taken away from us, and all of us sold into slavery, eh? We have longed for our homes and for schools to teach us, and they have laughed at us. All we have ever wanted was to be let alone to live and to work and make our country great, and we are tired—tired and sick of being cheated. . . ."

Outside in the dust, that whirled along under a sky of driving clouds, long lines of soldiers on horseback stood in the obscurity, while their officers passed along in front, peering closely at car- tridge belts and rifles.

"Geronimo," said a Captain to one trooper, "go back to the ammunition train and fill up the gaps in your *cartouchera*. You fool, you've been wasting your cartridges shooting coyotes!"

Across the desert westward toward the distant mountains rode strings of cavalry, the first to the front. About a thousand went, in ten different lines, diverging like wheel spokes; the jungle of their spurs ringing, their red-white-and-green flags floating straight out, crossed bandoliers gleaming dully, rifles flopping across their sad- dles, heavy, high sombreros and many-colored blankets.

Behind each company plodded ten or twelve women on foot, carrying cooking utensils on their heads and backs, and perhaps a pack mule loaded with sacks of corn. And as they passed the cars they shouted back to their friends on the trains.

"Poco tiempo California!" cried one.

"Oh! there's a *colorado* for you!" yelled another. "I'll bet you were with Salazar in Orozco's Revolution. Nobody ever said '*Poco tiempo California*' except Salazar when he was drunk!"

The other man looked sheepish. "Well, maybe I was," he admit- ted. "But wait till I get a shot at my old *compañeros*. I'll show you whether I'm a Maderista or not!"

A little Indian in the rear cried: "I know how much of a Maderista you are, Luisito. At the first taking of Torreon, Villa gave you the choice of turning your coat or getting a *cabronasso* or *balasso* through the head!" And, joshing and singing, they jogged southwest, became small, and finally faded into the dust.

Villa himself stood leaning against a car, hands in his pockets. He wore an old slouch hat, a dirty shirt without a collar, and a badly frayed and shiny brown suit. All over the dusty plain in front of him men and horses had sprung up like magic. There was an immense confusion of saddling and bridling—a cracked blowing of tin bugles. The Brigada Zaragosa was getting ready to leave camp—a flanking column of two thousand men who were to ride southeast and attack Tlahualilo and Sacramento. Villa, it seemed, had just arrived at Yermo. He had stopped off Monday night at Camargo to attend the wedding of a *compadre*. His face was drawn into lines of fatigue.

"*Carramba!*" he was saying with a grin, "we started dancing Monday evening, danced all night, all the next day, and last night, too! What a *baile*! And what *muchachas*! The girls of Camargo and Santa Rosalia are the most beautiful in Mexico! I am worn out—*rendido*! It was harder work than twenty battles. . . ."

ANITA DESAI

(1937–)

Anita Desai was born in Mussoorie, India; her father was Bengali and her mother, German. She was educated in English, and that is the language she uses to write her short stories and novels. She has been a Booker Prize nominee three times. Her books include *Fire on the Mountain* (1978), *Games at Twilight* (1979), *Clear Light of Day* (1980), *In Custody* (1984), *Baumgartner's Bombay* (1988), and *Journey to Ithaca* (1995). She is a professor at the MIT Program in Writing and Humanistic Studies.

Desai's novel *The Zigzag Way* (2004) was nominated for the Orange Prize for Fiction in 2005. It traces the journey of a postgraduate student studying immigrations. He follows his girlfriend, a scientist, to Mexico. While she follows her own studies, he searches for the history of his Cornish grandparents, who had been part of a community of Cornish miners relocated to this faraway, exotic place at a time when Zapata and Pancho Villa were leading revolutions. Through the characters he meets, world history intersects with his personal journey, and his search culminates when confronting his own family's past during Mexico's Day of the Dead.

There were times when Davey did make clear to Betty what he thought of her free ways. There was the occasion when the circus came to town, one of the many small, mangy circuses that traveled from village to village with its creaking wagons and brass band. The striped tent went up in a dusty field, the cages with their shabby lions and bears drawn into a circle. The hurdy-gurdy played its tunes excruciatingly, and spun sugar billowed out of a booth in sweet cumulus clouds of livid pink. A man in a clown's costume rode a donkey through the town, shouting, "See el Gran Hernandez pull a loaded wagon with his teeth! See la Bella Isadora ride a mighty elephant!" and Betty grew as excited as a child, as Lupe. "Oh, let's go," she cried, because at home, wouldn't she have caught her friends Agnes's and Sally's hands and gone running? But it appeared that in Mexico a Cornishwoman could not do that, go down to the Indian village and sit there with brown Mexican crowds. Davey's appalled look made that clear.

It was only the woman known to them as Tough Tansy, wife to the carpenter at the works and mother of five, who dressed her children up in their best and took them down as bold as could be, asking no one for permission. She kept her chin up and marched down the lane, herding her brood before her like a flock of goslings, and calling out to the women who watched from their doorways, "We're going to the circus—to see el Gran Hernandez eat fire and Issydora ride the ellyphant, aren't we, chicks? Come along!"

Davey said that it served Fred Barnstaple right for picking up a woman here in Mexico for a wife instead of fetching a proper one from Cornwall, and when Betty sulked over the sink and the dishes, he pointed out to her all the social activities provided for the miners' families by the Company, "like the picnic on the Duke of Cornwall's birthday." He was taken aback by Betty's fiery outburst at that.

"Oh yes," she said, hands on her hips, "that's one day your fine manager and his wife think of the miners up on the hill. Give us a tea treat with bacon sandwiches and feel proud when they see us fall on them like beggars. Then they can go back to their Casa Grande where none of us has ever so much as set foot."

"Now, Betty, I didn't think you'd care to visit them."

"I don't," she said, stamping her foot. "I don't. That is not what I meant and you know it, Davey Rowse."

But she gave her family an account of the occasion that

sounded happy enough. "Did you ever think," she wrote, "that here on a mountain in Mexico we would be celebrating the Duke of Cornwall's birthday?" They had been taken in wagons decorated with streamers down the steep hillside to a ledge where the picnic had been spread out under a great mesquite tree and games arranged for the children, races for the adults. When the sun began to sink, Davey came and pulled Betty to her feet, asking her to come and look at the view with him. It was one of those rare days when work and responsibility did not seem to weigh on him and make him dour, and Betty, delighted to see it, agreed.

They walked down to the edge where the land fell away in a sudden precipice to the valley and a lake where egrets stepped among the reeds, herons spread their wings to dry, and pelicans sailed along as if sliding across glass. He was pointing out the different birds to her when she noticed a large solitary hacienda built against the flank of the mountain already in shadow and so dark as to be barely discernible.

"And that?" she asked.

"Oh, that was a convent built by the Spanish priests who came to convert the Indians. The Mexicans threw them out after the War of Independence."

"So, is it empty? Did no one move in?"

"Actually, the Company did. They bought it and turned it into a kind of guesthouse for people on the board when they come to see the mines. 'Course, no one does. Come out here to the back of beyond to see the muck their fortunes come from? Not them," Davey said, looking at her because he knew she would approve of his tone. "It just lies empty. But when the president of Mexico came to open our electrical installation, he stayed there and the owners threw a banquet for him. They had chefs come from Mexico City to prepare his meals," Davey went on, providing the details he knew Betty enjoyed so much, "and an orchestra to play for him so he could dance with the ladies. Then he came up here to the mines and they lined the road with lanterns and trees hung with paper flowers. They lit bonfires on every hilltop and had a fireworks display to beat all fireworks. Just as if he was a king."

"A king in a fairy story," Betty said wonderingly. "We should go there one day." Glancing over her shoulder at the gathering under the tree, she added, "Just us, you and me."

He smiled and plucked a grass stalk to chew on. "How? We'd have to get a horse to take us. Shall we ride a horse together, Mrs. Rowse?"

The picture amused her. "Let's."

Holding hands, they strolled back to where the gathering had begun to sing Cornish songs, and when they got back and rejoined them, a toast was drunk to the duke—beer for the men, lemonade for the women and children. Then Betty helped the women pick up and fold and tidy away and the men got the wagons ready to take them back.

The occasion for that excursion never did arise, and shortly afterward Davey forbade Betty to go for walks alone on evenings when he was kept late at the mine, and he actually laid down the limits beyond which she must not go, even with Lupe.

Betty was puzzled. "What do you think might happen if I did?"

"I cannot tell and that is what I don't care for, not to know what might happen. All I know is it's not safe."

"And who told you that?"

"There's talk," he said. "Don't think everyone is so friendly as you think."

It displeased her that he should be suspicious of the people they lived among and whom she knew to be friendly and kind, for they unfailingly wished her a "*Buenos dias*" and a "*Buenas tardes*" when they passed her and never pulled a face or made a gesture that could be thought hostile. It made her wonder at Davey's new attitude—he was often dour but never unfair—and she demanded a reason for it.

He explained that there had been trouble at the mine: one of the *mineros,* Julio, was found to have gone down the hill into town to buy kerosene for his lantern and corn for his family at the general store, not at the Tienda de Raya run by the Company. The manager, a Scotsman named MacDuff, had him hauled up and warned. When he defied the manager and did it again, saying he would go wherever the prices were fair, he was discharged and a wave of anger and resentment went through the community that Betty imagined was so harmonious. Did not all the men play football together, Scots and Cornish and Mexican? Were they not equally excited about the centennial celebrations to come? Now this was shown to be a sham, nothing but a front for what was unacceptable.

Putting down her knife and fork, she exploded, "And isn't any of you standing up for him? For shame!"

When Davey kept silent and did not openly agree with her, she went on, "Don't you think it's wrong? These poor people being made to hand over what they earn back to the Company? By *order?*"

"It's not as simple as that, Betty."

"Oh but it is," she insisted, "it is."

In Mexico City the centennial of the Revolution was inaugurated by President Díaz. They heard of banquets at the Palacio Nacional where French cuisine was prepared for the guests and an orchestra of more than a hundred musicians played the president's favorite waltz, "El Abandonado," under thousands of electric lights. At one such ball, he announced his intention to stand for a ninth term as president. At the same occasion he handed out ninety-nine-year concessions of copper, oil, and lead to the Americans Morgan, Guggenheim, Rockefeller, and Hearst.

Such news reassured all the foreigners who had begun to grow worried, and so celebrations came even to their dusty scrapheap of a town. The miners and their families were taken down to hear the *grito*, the stirring call for independence that had been made by the priest Miguel Hidalgo way back in 1810. It was read out now on the balcony of the town hall by the mayor in his polished and buttoned and gleaming best. A band played, there was a parade of floats from which beauties in Spanish dress tossed roses to the crowds, buntings and streamers blew from every lamppost, and in the evening there were fireworks in the plaza for which the entire town turned out, Mexican and Cornish alike. When they came to an end, in drifting parasols of smoke, the night sky, clearing, revealed a pale band that seemed to be the ghost of a streaking rocket. Only it did not speed away and die. It remained because it was Halley's comet. Everyone had heard what it portended but no one wished to say on that night. Even the mines were shut and silent, no whistle blew to remind them they were there. Instead, all turned to tables loaded with great earthenware bowls filled with food simmering in sauces and gravies.

Betty turned away and asked to be taken home. Davey was con-cerned because it was not like her to refuse anything unusual or pleasurable. He suggested, at home, that she have a glass of milk or a slice of fruit. Pulling a face at the pineapple in the bowl on the table, she turned away, saying, "I'd give a lot for a fresh juicy apple off a tree."

"Why, what's wrong?" Davey asked in surprise. "I never heard you say no to a pineapple before."

She merely shook her head. The truth was that she had even stopped going to the market—its sights and aromas now made her feel quite ill. There had been a time she had wandered by mis-take into a lane lined with booths where herbal remedies were sold. The bunches of dried herbs and roots had not been so bad but there were objects that mystified her—raccoon tails, squirrel pelts, dried puffers and devilfish, even a stuffed alligator and a string of emerald hummingbirds. These were all very dead and harmless but under the tables some sacks moved with mysterious life and the tail of an iguana protruded from one, the snout of an armadillo from another, making her rush away, with Lupe laughing at her squeamishness.

Davey reacted with his usual equanimity, explaining these were the ingredients used by the witch doctors to cure various sicknesses and ailments. "There's no hospital around here, you know."

"I hope I'm not ever ill here, Davey," she said shuddering.

"Just don't go there again," he advised reasonably.

"I won't," she said, but there had been the boy who had followed her, holding in one hand a lit candle, in the other a bottle. When he saw her looking at them, he held the lit candle under the bottle and that was when she saw it contained a live scorpion. Shocked as she was, she could not tear herself away and watched, in horror, as the scorpion raised its tail over its head and stung itself to death. Laughing into her face, the boy held out his hand and demanded a peso before Lupe could push him away.

She neither told Davey nor wrote home of it.

The tempo, the tenor of life on the mountain and around the mine began to change as news filtered in—that a General Madero had declared an end to thirty years of Porfirio Díaz's rule, that the president had fled to the United States. All of this was incredible to those who had not known anything or anyone else in power for all or most of their lives. Then stories began to buzz like swarming bees, of Emiliano Zapata in the south, and Pancho Villa in the north. Zapata had once cleaned horse dung from floors of Carrara marble in President Díaz's stables, it was said, and now led a troop of mounted Indians against his troops. As for Pancho Villa, he was never without a gun at all, saying, "For me the war began when I was born." New heroes for new times: their stories began to acquire a reality, and immediacy.

Then the *mineros* began to disappear from their own mine, without a word. When the manager sent for them, it was to find their huts abandoned, thorn bushes stacked in the open doorways. They had been recruited—some by the rebels, others by the federals—and gone to fight for their country. Their women had gone with them, *soldaderas* of the Revolution. The village on the hill below the Cornishmen's cottages had only a few old people left in it, to mind the children and some whining hungry dogs.

The railroad trains that President Díaz had only lately inaugurated still creaked and rattled over the vast plains of Mexico. They had escorts of armed guards, but were watched by men in sombreros from behind the red and purple rocks of the sierra. Whistles sounded in the stillness, accentuating the silence.

Tiqui-taca, rucu-raca . . .

Then there was a night when the hills, usually silent mounds of darkness, echoed with a sudden volley of shots, shocking and splintering. When the men went out to see what was happening, they saw flames leaping up over a neighboring mine on a distant hilltop—it might have been a celebratory bonfire. At dawn the news came that the rebels, the *insurgentes*, had looted the warehouse, emptied the vaults, and, after tying up whoever they found on the premises, vanished along with the Company's mules. There was panic at the news. "*Insurgentes?*" people asked. "From where?" And some went over to release the trussed manager and supervisor and assess the damage. A party of federals rode into the town soon after—grim, dusty, saddled officers of the government—asking for leads. Had anyone seen the rebels? No? They were warned to be on guard and report.

Everyone watched constantly. By daylight, a cloud of dust raised along a path could give away the approach of troops—rebels or federals—but by night there was no such sign; they could only strain their ears for the telltale clatter of hoofs or a shot and the hiss that followed a bullet. Men stayed up at night, smoking, drinking, playing cards, waiting.

They were to wait for the hoot of an owl. "An *owl?*" Betty asked when told. It would be a man, Davey informed her, with the message: "*La muerte viene con el tecolote.*" Betty thought that was the foolishness of grown men playing boys' games. "Death comes with an owl!" she sniffed.

Older men, who had been in the mining towns in the desert and the sierra for decades already, recalled the raids of the Comanches and the Apaches. This, too, made Betty sniff. "Comanches! Scalp hunters! They've been hearing too many of those Wild West stories, I think."

Ignoring her scorn, when he was put on a night shift, Davey engaged a boy, Lupe's brother, to keep guard over the house. Betty could not sleep for the awareness of his presence on their doorstep.

She begged Davey to send him away. "Then I'll have to send you to San Luis Potosí for safety. Some of the women have already gone," he told her, and when she opened her mouth to protest, added, "You can't take risks, Betty, in your condition."

It was the first time they had referred to her "condition." Betty shrank from the word, and recovered only to say, "And you? What about you taking risks? Aren't you the father?"

They stared at each other in bewilderment, each wanting to make something of this moment, something memorable. Instead, neither could make the gesture: it was not the moment for one so private.

GRAHAM GREENE

(1904–91)

Prolific novelist and travel writer Graham Greene was also a devoted Catholic. In the 1930s Greene traveled to Mexico in order to report firsthand on the official campaign there against the Catholic Church that followed the Mexican Revolution. He set out to chronicle persecution of clergy members and churchgoers in Tabasco and Chiapas. He writes about abandoned and burned churches, the salve of religion for the impoverished, and the clandestine lives of priests who secretly celebrated Mass and other religious rituals.

Greene disliked almost everything about Mexico—the food, the people, and the landscape. His entire journey reads like a self-imposed penance. When he's leaving Veracruz for Tabasco, several people tell him not to ride the particular steamship he has booked passage on (in fact, the fare includes life insurance). He still insists on taking it and, not surprisingly, is miserable. Instead of waiting for a plane to travel from Tabasco to Chiapas, he mounts a mule and leaves for the mountainous route in a downpour. Despite his peevishness, *Another Mexico* (1939) (published as *The Lawless Roads* in England) is a fascinating and thoughtful record of a unique time in Mexico, when a deeply religious country outlawed religion.

THE GULF

There were no sex divisions in the dark cabin: in the bunk below me a woman lay for the whole forty-two hours, never stirring, never eating. A young school teacher was on my left hand; his shelf, when he went on deck, was littered with pamphlets—about the petroleum dispute, about the Church. He lent them to the sailors—you came on a sailor bunched by the lifeboat absorbed in the President's message to the people. All the time the companies were appealing to the Supreme Court and the Labour Board was arguing its case the presses must have been busy with that message; long before the Supreme Court decided in favour of the workers and the companies refused to implement the award, long before expropriation was announced, the President had his message in type. It followed me everywhere: it was read out in remote Chiapas inns.

The boat rolled horribly all night. I wondered if the wind was from the north, but I no longer cared. It is before you cross a frontier that you experience fear. Now I lay there in my clothes, on my wooden shelf, with dim curiosity and wonder. It was too bizarre and inexplicable—rolling on a Mexican barge across the Gulf. Why? On my right hand the younger girl lay on her face, her legs exposed up to the thighs by the dusty light of the globe outside. The school teacher began a gentle flirtation in a protective way: he lent her a copy of the President's message and she lent him a cheap song-book: they hummed to each other softly in the oily night. My riding-boots, for which there was no room in my suitcase, rolled in a composite mass with the packet of ham, the sun helmet, and my electric torch.

In the morning I got on deck. The Atlantic rollers rode in under a grey cold sky. The girls' brother lay with sick abandon on a straw mat. A folding table was opened, and breakfast was handed up through a hatch in the deck from the engine-room—a loaf of bread and a plate of anonymous fish scraps from which the eyeballs stood mournfully out. I couldn't face it, and rashly made my way down to the only privy: a horrible cupboard in the engine-room with no ventilation, no flushing, and the ordure of I don't know how many days and voyages. That finished me for the rest of the day; I lay on my shelf through the morning and the afternoon and struggled up only once more before night.

And next morning everything was worse—not better. The sun was out and sucked out all the smells there were on the little ancient barge. Twice I dashed for the privy and the second time the whole door came off in my hands and fell on to the engine-room floor. Then in the late morning we came into smoother water and I got up on to the deck again—twenty feet of it on either side the smokestack, with two benches long enough to hold perhaps a dozen people. The captain stood in the bows with a toothpick in his hair, and everywhere you moved you found sailors doing up their trousers. The coast was in sight—a long low line of trees and sand like West Africa. I ate a ship's biscuit—there seemed to be cause for celebration. Thirst, though, was greater than hunger, but there was no beer nor mineral water on board; at meal times they made a shocking kind of coffee, but otherwise there was only the dubious water in a tin filter above the wash-basin, and that ran out completely after twelve hours.

FRONTERA

We arrived at Frontera at two-fifteen, forty-one hours from Veracruz, in an appalling heat. Only, I think, in Monrovia had I experienced its equal, but Frontera like Monrovia is freshened a little by the sea. To know how hot the world can be I had to wait for Villahermosa. Shark fins glided like periscopes at the entrance to the Grijalva River, the scene of the Conquistadores' first landing in Mexico, before they sailed on to Veracruz. Frontera itself was out of sight round a river bend; three or four aerials stuck up into the blazing sky from among the banana groves and the palm-leaf huts: it was like Africa seeing itself in a mirror across the Atlantic. Little islands of lily plants came floating down from the interior, and the carcasses of old stranded steamers held up the banks.

And then round a bend in the river Frontera, the frontier. So it will remain to me, though the Tabascan authorities have renamed it Puerto Obregón: the Presidencia and a big warehouse and a white blanched street running off between wooden shacks—hairdressers and the inevitable dentists, but no cantinas anywhere, for there is prohibition in Tabasco. No intoxicant is allowed but beer, and that costs a peso a bottle—a ruinous price in Mexico. The lily plants floated by; the river divided round a green island half a mile from shore, and the vultures came flocking out, with little idiot heads and dusty serrated wings, to rustle round the shrouds. There was an election on: the name Bartlett occurred everywhere, and a red star. The soldiers stood in the shade of the Presidencia and watched us edge in against the river bank.

This was Tabasco—Garrido Canabal's isolated swampy puritanical state. Garrido—so it was said—had destroyed every church; he had organised a militia of Red Shirts, even leading them across the border into Chiapas in his hunt for a church or a priest. Private houses were searched for religious emblems, and prison was the penalty for possessing them. A young man I met in Mexico City—a family friend of Garrido's—was imprisoned three days for wearing a cross under his shirt; the dictator was incorruptible. A journalist on his way to photograph Tabasco was shot dead in Mexico City airport before he took his seat. Every priest was hunted down or shot, except one who existed for ten years in the forests and the swamps, venturing out only at night; his few letters, I was told, recorded an awful sense of impotence—to live in constant danger and yet be able to do so little, it hardly seemed worth the horror. Now Garrido is in Costa Rica, but his policy goes on . . . The customs officers came on board, their revolver holsters creaking as they climbed the rotting rail. I remembered a bottle of brandy in my suitcase.

Their search was not a formality. They not only went through the cargo but the captain's cabin: you could see them peering under his bunk. They felt in the lifeboat and insisted on having unlocked the little cupboard where the plates and knives were kept. Presently the passengers were summoned below to open their boxes; I allowed myself to forget all my Spanish. People came and explained things with their fingers. I could hold out no longer and went down. But the customs men had come to the end of their tether; the heat in the cabin was terrific; everybody was wedged together—I slipped quietly away again and nobody minded. On the quay they were unloading beer—it was our main cargo: a hundred and fifty dozen bottles, to be sold only by Government agents. Puritanism pays.

I went for a walk on shore; nothing to be seen but one little dusty plaza with fruit-drink stalls and a bust of Obregón on a pillar, two dentists' and a hairdresser's. The vultures squatted on the roofs. It was like a place besieged by scavengers—sharks in the river and vultures in the streets.

One introduction I had here, to the merchant who owned the warehouse on the quay, an old man with a little pointed beard who spoke no English. I told him I wanted to go to Palenque from Villahermosa. He tried to dissuade me—it was only a hundred miles, but it might take a week. First, as there were no roads for more than a few miles outside the capital I should have to return to Frontera, then I'd have to wait till I could get a barge up another river to Montecristo—or Zapata, as it was now called. There I could get horses. But the river journey would take two or three days and conditions would be—horrible. After all, I said, I had endured the *Ruiz Cano.* The *Ruiz Cano*, the old man said, was a fine boat . . . I went back to the ship discouraged. They were still unloading beer; they wouldn't be moving that night, for it was still ten hours to Villahermosa and they needed daylight for the passage.

At sunset the mosquitoes began—a terrifying steady hum like that of a sewing-machine. There were only two choices: to be eaten on deck (and probably catch malaria) or to go below to the

cabin and the appalling heat. The only porthole was closed for
fear of marauders; mosquito-nets seemed to shut out all the air
that was left. It was only eight o'clock. I lay naked under the net
and sweated; every ten minutes I tried to dry myself with a towel.
I fell asleep and woke again and fell asleep. Then somewhere I
heard a voice talking English—hollow overcivilised English, not
American. I thought I heard the word "interpreter." It must have
been a dream, and yet I can still remember that steady cultured
voice going on, and the feel of my own wet skin, the hum of mosquitoes, and my watch saying 10:32.

ANN LOUISE BARDACH

Ann Louise Bardach is the author of *Cuba Confidential: Love and Vengeance in Miami and Havana* (2003), which was a finalist for the New York Public Library Bernstein Award for Excellence in Journalism and the PEN/USA Award for Best Nonfiction, and named one of Ten Best Books of 2002 by the *Los Angeles Times*. Bardach has a reputation as a fearless investigative reporter whether she's interviewing Fidel Castro in Havana or his enemies in Miami, defending the rights of women in Islamic countries, or heading into war zones to conduct interviews with rebel leaders. She was a staff writer for *Vanity Fair* for ten years and has since written for *The New York Times, Washington Post, Los Angeles Times,* and *Slate*. She won the PEN/USA Award for Journalism in 1994 for her reporting on Mexican politics.

In this essay, excerpted from the article she wrote for *Vanity Fair* in 1994, she tracks down the elusive Subcomandante Marcos, a leader of the Zapatista National Liberation Army in Chiapas. This small army made up of indigenous people caught the world's attention when they rose up in arms against the Mexican government. Though the armed conflict was short-lived, the battle was also fought with words. Subcomandante Marcos's letters chastising the government and defending the poor of Chiapas were written with both poetic style and political acumen, making him a hero to many in Latin America as a defender of the dispossessed. The fact that he was masked and refused to reveal his identity and background only added allure to his persona.

Excerpted from "MEXICO'S POET REBEL:
SUBCOMANDANTE MARCOS AND MEXICO
IN CHAOS," in
Vanity Fair, *July 1994:*

*"We fight for the land and not for illusions that give us nothing to
eat. With or without elections, the people are chewing the cud of bit-
terness."*

Emiliano Zapata, 1879–1919

*"The government says that this is not an indigenous uprising, but we
think that if thousands of indigenous people rise up in protest, then
it is indeed an indigenous uprising."*

Subcomandante Marcos,
Zapatista Communique
January 6, 1994

"*No hay paso. Ordenes del Comite. Lo Siento,*" the handwritten note
read. "You can't come through. Orders from the Committee. I'm
sorry." It was signed, in his inimitable scrawl, "Subcomandante
Marcos." True, I couldn't say I hadn't been warned. The previous
night I had bumped into a claque of reporters outside the cathedral in San Cristobal de las Casas. Three of them had just spent
three days outside this same camp tap-dancing for an interview
with Marcos, the leader of the revolutionaries who call themselves
the Zapatista National Liberation Army. "He's not giving any
more," one of them told me. "He says it's too dangerous now."
"Now" referred to the national climate of electrified shock and
horror following the assassination two days earlier, on March 23,
of the de facto next president of Mexico, Luis Donaldo Colosio.
It was widely whispered that Colosio—like Caesar—had met his
death at the hands of those closest to him. Only nine days before

that, financier Alfredo Harp Helu, the president of Mexico's largest bank and a close associate and friend of President Carlos Salinas de Gortari's, had been the latest kidnapping victim, held for a $50 million ransom. Suddenly, Mexico was reeling. Kidnappings and political assassinations—all on the heels of a grassroots revolution in January that burst out in Chiapas, a state so poor, so desperate, that according to the writer Carlos Fuentes, "even the rocks are screaming."

The ominous tone of Marcos's note was unmistakable, particularly the last line: "On another occasion, *if there is one*, we will have the honor of attending to you in the manner you deserve." I read it again and passed it to Medea Benjamin, founder and director of Global Exchange, a humanitarian-aid group based in San Francisco. Medea, who weighs less than 100 pounds and speaks six languages, had her own agenda, which included arranging for the delivery of machetes desperately needed by the local farmers to replace those confiscated by the army. I had suggested we travel together, knowing that her presence could only improve my chances.

I nudged her away from the three skinny, ski-masked, rifle-toting Zapatistas who had, upon our arrival, ordered us to wait in an abandoned one-room schoolhouse perched on a hill. The village of La Garrucha sits in the Lacondon rain forest, not far from the Guatemalan border. Getting there had required dodging six army checkpoints, not to mention two Zapatista shakedowns once we had entered the rebel-held neutral zone of San Miguel.

I knew Marcos had to be close by. His response to my request to see him had come back in minutes. Urgently, we sat down and scratched out letters of appeal, which we gave to the messengers. Ten minutes later they returned. No interview, they said, and they wanted the provisions—including 20 liters of gasoline—that Medea had kindly brought for them. They even demanded that we take back some reporters who were stranded nearby.

Hot, tired, and furious, I stormed out of the schoolhouse with Medea and headed over to the Zapatistas' convoy truck parked down the road. A soldier bolted out of nowhere and waved his machine gun for us to go back. Instead, we plopped down on the grass, careful to avoid a second encounter with a *cuatro narices*, one of the deadliest snakes in the world, which calls this region home. Fifteen minutes later, the same Zapatista was running toward us, "*Venga! Venga!*" he yelled. Baffled, we followed, and halfway down the dusty road I saw him. Sitting under an ancient, craggy tree between two clusters of thatched huts, surrounded by three masked Zapatistas, their automatic weapons slicing the humid air in front of them, was Marcos, puffing on his pipe, looking as serene as the Buddha.

"I am a brilliant myth," Marcos has said, in response to the ceaseless rumors and hype about him. However, framed by the wild pigs, ducks, and hens grazing on the soft hills behind him, he looked the very stuff of myth. Indeed, it seemed hard to believe that this vision of bucolic contentment had engineered the first post–cold war revolution.

January 1 was supposed to have been a day of celebration in Mexico over the enactment of President Salinas's fiercely won NAFTA agreement. Mexico was supposed to have become a First World country. At least, that's what the government had been saying, and some Mexicans were actually starting to believe it. Instead, a previously unheard-of brigade of thousands of armed Indians burst out of the jungle and seized seven cities and towns in Chiapas. Suddenly, the world was reminded by this remarkably organized and efficient band of Mayan Indians in shabby, home-made uniforms that there was another Mexico, the one in which nearly half the population lives below the poverty line.

Within days, the rebels had liberated nearly 200 prison inmates, trashed several police interrogation centers, seized a haul of armaments and ammunition, and burned the records in a half dozen town halls and courthouses. In their greatest show of symbolic stagecraft, the rebels kidnapped General Absalón Castellanos Dominguez, the former governor of Chiapas, whose family has ruled the region for decades as if it were their private fiefdom. For forty-five days, the Zapatistas detained Castellanos, subjecting him to a people's trial, and finding him guilty of crimes from plunder to murder. Then, in a grand gesture of reverse noblesse oblige, they released him, unharmed.

Caught utterly by surprise, the military awoke with a fury. Within a week they had brutally retaken the area. The local Catholic diocese estimates that more than 400 people—mostly civilians—were killed. Although a truce was called and subsequent peace talks with the Zapatistas have shown some promise of reconciliation, Chiapas today is an armed camp, with anguish and anxiety palpable everywhere.

On January 10, Mexican newspapers received the first communiqué from a man calling himself Subcomandante Marcos. It began: "Here we are, the dead of all times, dying once again, but now with the objective of living." By week's end, Marcos had conquered the international media just as he had taken Chiapas. He was hailed as Robin Hood, the Lone Ranger, Geronimo, the "first postmodern guerilla hero," even the reincarnation of his movement's namesake, Emiliano Zapata, the revolutionary Mexican peasant leader who was tricked into an army ambush, but who some insist never died.

"This is no ordinary politician," confessed Juan Enriquez Cabot, one of the government's negotiating team. "He moved [people] to tears." He also reduced the normally cynical press corps to a pack of groupies. Each week pilgrimages of reporters trek into the jungle, sometimes waiting more than a week before Marcos deigns to address them en masse. At a dinner party in

Mexico City in March, which included Carlos Fuentes and Gabriel García Márquez, one guest argued that Marcos had to be "at least three people," owing to his prolific missives to the press, often eight-page typed "communiqués" of revolutionary fervor leavened with wit, humor, and even poetry, which have enthralled Mexicans nearly as much as their soap operas do. Another guest, citing the erudition in the communiqués, insisted that, "Marcos is one of us," meaning a member of the intelligentsia. "I'm sure he was a priest," Carlos Monsiváis, one of Mexico's preeminent writers, told me. "At the very least, he went to divinity school. You can see it in his writings, his thinking." What is certain is that in the mythological pantheon of revolutionary heroes, Subcomandante Marcos has secured a niche for himself, inching toward Che Guevara, and that Mexico—perhaps all of Latin America—will never be the same again.

The genius of the Zapatistas has been in their insistence on being a 100-percent homegrown peasant revolt—so bereft of stale ideological rant or rhetoric that even their adversaries have grudgingly conceded that their demands for social, electoral, and land reforms are legitimate. Moreover, they have struck a chord that resonates with Mexicans of all classes and regions, Mexicans disgusted by a country ruled since time immemorial by the *mordida*, or bribe. Two weeks after the Zapatista siege, a crowd estimated at 100,000 marched on the Zócalo in Mexico City in support of the insurgents, followed by dozens of demonstrations on April 10, the 75th anniversary of the death of Zapata. And when Verdi's opera *Nabucco* was presented in Mexico City's august Palacio de las Bellas Artes in early February, the audience jumped to its feet when the chorus sang about rebellion, and chanted, "Viva Zapata! Viva Chiapas!"

"Look, I'm sorry," Marcos began, speaking in hushed Spanish, "but it's too dangerous for you to be here." He explained how the murder of Colosio had changed everything, how the Zapatistas would certainly be blamed for it, and how the Mexican army was closing in on the guerillas. An attack was imminent, he said, adding grimly, "the army, no doubt, will kill you and then blame that too on the Zapatistas." He motioned to the planes passing overhead, and said that since Colosio's assassination more than fifty military planes flew overhead every day. "It's just too dangerous," he said, waving toward the hills behind him, "to take you back there to talk."

Then, I wondered, couldn't we talk right where we were? He paused, smiled, and agreed to talk "for a few minutes." More than four hours later, as darkness was falling, I turned off my tape recorder. During that time, Marcos never removed his light wool black ski mask. However, the mask was amply stretched, and it frequently revealed more of his face than it concealed. In fact, the mask seems to enhance his good features and blur his imperfections. He appears to be hovering near forty. His legendary green eyes are actually hazel, and while he is not an Indian, he is olive-complected. His nose is broad and his skin has deep pores. A short, dark beard flecked with white is visible around his mouth, but his arms and upper chest are virtually hairless. Most striking, however, considering the fury unleashed by his ragtag army, is his manner—one of gentleness. At times his voice is so soft that he is barely audible. It is his resolute convictions combined with a seemingly imperturbable serenity that has convinced many that he is a renegade *padre*. Marcos has denied it, joking that he hasn't been to Mass since he was eight.

Marcos is smaller than he appears in photographs, amplified by layers of clothing and gear. Though the Lacondon rain forest can sizzle during the day, temperatures have been known to drop to freezing at night. This day it was warm and humid, but Marcos seemed unbothered by his heavy uniform: a long-sleeved brown cotton shirt over a black T-shirt, black jeans, and combat boots. Tied loosely around his neck was a burnt-orange paisley bandana, the official garment of the Zapatistas. Two bandoliers of ammunition crisscrossed his chest, dangling above his pistol and his automatic rifle, and on top of his ski mask, he wore a tattered beige cap with three faded red stars on the brim.

He effusively offered thanks for the gasoline. "It's like gold to us," he said, expressing amazement that it made it through the army roadblocks. Any supplies that the army judges useful to the Zapatistas are often confiscated, the military's strategy being to force the rebels out of the designated neutral zone mandated by the peace talks. When they go into town—Ocosingo to the north or Altamirano to the south—to buy things, Marcos said, they risk their lives. "They have some of our names," he explained. "and if they find your name on the *lista negra,* the blacklist, you won't be seen again. Four of our people disappeared at the checkpoint in Ocosingo—after the peace process was already under way. To us, this is a sign that they want to provoke us so that we will be forced to respond and then they will have an excuse to attack us."

Marcos offered up a nightmare scenario for the United States if the Mexican government fails to achieve an agreement with the Zapatistas. Claiming that civil war in Mexico will be inevitable if the government retreats from the peace talks, he warned that a dire immigration crisis would result. Already, he said, more than 20,000 people have fled their homes. "What would happen with immigration to the United States if the war spread out of Chiapas? Chiapas has about 3 million people and Mexico has 90 million . . . More than 40 million live in poverty. If there is civil war in Mexico, it doesn't matter how big or thick you construct that wall, the wall along the U.S. border will come down."

When I told him that Americans in general seem to be sympathetic toward the Mexican insurgents, he seemed relieved. "That's very good news," he says, "because the U.S. government doesn't do anything without first looking at what the American people are thinking. Not since Vietnam," he added knowingly. "Now before the United States intervenes somewhere, it takes a survey of public opinion like it did in the Persian Gulf War." Clearly the possibility of American military intervention—either overt or covert—has weighed upon him.

To that end, the Zapatista agenda of agrarian and social reform has been carefully crafted. So far the insurgents have dodged being labeled "communists," *Fidelistas,* or Sandinistas. "The bogeyman of the American people were the communists. They were the ones that ate children. There is no more communism in the world," Marcos said. "Fidel Castro? He has a lot of problems in his own country. The Salvadorans? The Nicaraguans? The Left is out of power. So what is behind this revolution in Mexico? We don't want power. We don't want money. Just our land back. The land that was ours and taken from us by the *ganaderos* [ranchers]. And democracy. There is no democracy. You cannot vote for an alternative. Well, you can vote, but it doesn't mean anything." He was referring to Mexico's staggering history of electoral fraud, notably the presidential victory of Salinas and his party, the Institutional Revolutionary Party (PRI), in 1988. (In 1992, the rebel stronghold of Ocosingo reported a shocking tally of 100 percent for the PRI.) "This leads to lots of problems—political repression, jailings, killings," Marcos said drolly. "So in this kind of struggle, the communist bogeyman cannot be invoked." Like a seasoned debater, he addressed, unprompted, America's other obsession to the south. "There is another bogeyman—drug smuggling. They can say, 'There is no cold war, but this is a drug war.' But in our army, in our territory, no drugs are being grown." He waves his hand toward his soldiers, all pencil-thin Indians, most of them under twenty. "You can see that our army is not a rich one. We don't have guns or good equipment."

What the Zapatistas do have is five centuries of simmering rage of being lied to, tricked, and marginalized. After the conquistadors arrived in the early 1500s, there was actually a lively debate as to whether the Indians were in fact human beings with souls. According to the Spanish chronicler Bartolomé de las Casas, Mayans and Aztecs were tortured and killed for sport. Today, some argue, things haven't changed all that much. Making up roughly 15 percent of the population, Mexico's 14 million Indians are its poorest citizens in every respect. La Garrucha, like most Indian villages, has no running water or electricity. There is no gas and no sewage system. Marcos said that more than 150,000 Indian children have died from preventable diseases in the last decade, and that 75 percent of the Indian population is illiterate. I asked him if he meant in Spanish or in the four commonly used Indian languages: Tzotzil, Tzeltal, Tojolobal, and Chol. "In everything," he said. But, he added, "we see how quickly they learn, how well they understand things. Our soldiers, who don't speak Spanish, are able to put together a gun. We receive pieces of guns and they keep fooling around until they put it together. These people have a lot to teach us."

Marcos seemed bemused by his new fame. He grinned with embarrassment when he leafed through a stack of clippings that described him as Mexico's newest sex symbol. "Sex symbol!" he said, laughing like a schoolboy. "If I took the mask off, it would be much worse because I am so good-looking." Ironically, the Zapatista ideal of anonymity—the masks not only conceal them from their enemies, but are intended to maintain egalitarianism among the ranks—has, in fact, backfired. The hottest-selling items in Mexico today are Marcos T-shirts, Marcos dolls, Marcos key rings. Other Zapatista soldiers—Moises, Ramona, Arturo, Yolanda—have also become celebrities, but on a much smaller scale. "Right now you can't individualize Marcos," he said, "but without a mask I would be individualized. When I am killed, someone else will simply put on my mask and continue being Marcos." At best, it is a lofty conceit; in reality, it is delusional. There could never be a convincing imitation of this unique creature.

DOWN AND OUT
IN MEXICO

Desperados

TENNESSEE WILLIAMS

(1 9 1 1 – 8 3)

One of America's most renowned playwrights, Tennessee Williams achieved early success with his plays about volatile, passion-driven characters. *The Glass Menagerie* (1945) and *A Streetcar Named Desire* (1947), which won the Pulitzer Prize, made him famous. He went on to write many more plays, including *Night of the Iguana* in 1961. This tale of a defrocked minister embroiled in a sex scandal won Williams the New York Drama Critics Award.

John Huston directed the film version of *Night of the Iguana* in Puerto Vallarta, Mexico, in 1964. The star-studded cast, including Ava Gardner and Richard Burton, transfigured the small, sleepy seaside village. The affair between Burton and Elizabeth Taylor—both at the time married to other people—injected glamour and a forbidden allure to the picturesque town. Although it still maintains the cobblestone roads and offers the same beautiful beaches it had then, Puerto Vallarta has grown into a thriving tourist destination. Some claim *Night of the Iguana*, a tale of searching and escape, is what transformed it.

△▽

The play takes place in the summer of 1940 in a rather rustic and very Bohemian hotel, the Costa Verde, which, as its name implies, sits on a jungle-covered hilltop overlooking the "caleta," or "morning beach" of Puerto Barrio in Mexico. But this is decidedly not the Puerto Barrio of today. At that time—twenty years ago—the west coast of Mexico had not yet become the Las Vegas and Miami Beach of Mexico. The villages were still predominantly primitive Indian villages, and the still-water morning beach of Puerto Barrio and the rain forests above it were among the world's wildest and loveliest populated places.

The setting for the play is the wide verandah of the hotel. This roofed verandah, enclosed by a railing, runs around all four sides of the somewhat dilapidated tropical-style frame structure, but on the stage we see only the front and one side. Below the verandah, which is slightly raised above the stage level, are shrubs with vivid trumpet-shaped flowers and a few cactus plants, while at the sides we see the foliage of the encroaching jungle. A tall coconut palm slants upward at one side, its trunk notched for a climber to chop down coconuts for rum-cocos. In the back wall of the verandah are the doors of a line of small cubicle bedrooms which are screened with mosquito-net curtains. For the night scenes they are lighted from within, so that each cubicle appears as a little interior stage, the curtains giving a misty effect to their dim inside lighting. A path which goes down through the rain forest to the highway and the beach, its opening masked by foliage, leads off from one side of the verandah. A canvas hammock is strung from posts on the verandah and there are a few old wicker rockers and rattan lounging chairs at one side.

ACT ONE

As the curtain rises, there are sounds of a party of excited female tourists arriving by bus on the road down the hill below the Costa Verde Hotel. MRS. MAXINE FAULK, *the proprietor of the hotel, comes around the turn of the verandah. She is a stout, swarthy woman in her middle forties—affable and rapaciously lusty. She is wearing a pair of Levi's and a blouse that is half unbuttoned. She is followed by* PEDRO, *a Mexican of about twenty—slim and attractive. He is an employee in the hotel and also her casual lover.* PEDRO *is stuffing his shirt under the belt of his pants and sweating as if he had been working hard in the sun.* MRS. FAULK *looks down the hill and is pleased by the sight of someone coming up from the tourist bus below.*

MAXINE [*calling out*]: Shannon! [*A man's voice from below answers: "Hi!"*] Hah! [MAXINE *always laughs with a single harsh, loud bark, open-*

ing her mouth like a seal expecting a fish to be thrown to it.] My spies told me that you were back under the border! [*to* PEDRO] Anda, hombre, anda!

[MAXINE'S *delight expands and vibrates in her as* SHANNON *labors up the hill to the hotel. He does not appear on the jungle path for a minute or two after the shouting between them starts.*]

MAXINE: Hah! My spies told me you went through Saltillo last week with a busload of women—a whole busload of females, all females, hah! How many you laid so far? Hah!

SHANNON [*from below, panting*]: Great Caesar's ghost . . . stop . . . shouting!

MAXINE: No wonder your ass is draggin', hah!

SHANNON: Tell the kid to help me up with this bag.

MAXINE [*shouting directions*]: Pedro! Anda—la maléta. Pancho, no seas flojo! Va y trae el equipaje del señor.

[PANCHO, *another young Mexican, comes around the verandah and trots down the jungle path.* PEDRO *has climbed up a coconut tree with a machete and is chopping down nuts for rum-cocos.*]

SHANNON [*shouting, below*]: Fred? Hey, Fred!

MAXINE [*with a momentary gravity*]: Fred can't hear you, Shannon. [*She goes over and picks up a coconut, shaking it against her ear to see if it has milk in it.*]

SHANNON [*still below*]: Where is Fred—gone fishing?

[MAXINE *lops the end off a coconut with the machete, as* PANCHO *trots up to the verandah with* SHANNON'S *bag—a beat-up Gladstone covered with travel stickers from all over the world. Then* SHANNON *appears, in a crumpled white linen suit. He is panting, sweating, and wild-eyed. About thirty-five,* SHANNON *is "black Irish." His nervous state is terribly apparent; he is a young man who has cracked up before and is going to crack up again—perhaps repeatedly.]*

MAXINE: Well! Lemme look at you!

SHANNON: Don't look at me, get dressed!

MAXINE: Gee, you look like you had it!

SHANNON: You look like you been having it, too. Get dressed!

MAXINE: Hell, I'm dressed. I never dress in September. Don't you know I never dress in September?

SHANNON: Well, just, just—button your shirt up.

MAXINE: How long you been off it, Shannon?

SHANNON: Off what?

MAXINE: The wagon . . .

SHANNON: Hell, I'm dizzy with fever. Hundred and three this morning in Cuernavaca.

MAXINE: Watcha got wrong with you?

SHANNON: Fever . . . fever . . . Where's Fred?

MAXINE: Dead.

SHANNON: Did you say *dead*?

MAXINE: That's what I said. Fred is dead.

SHANNON: How?

MAXINE: Less'n two weeks ago, Fred cut his hand on a fishhook, it got infected, infection got in his bloodstream, and he was dead inside of forty-eight hours. [*to* PANCHO] Vete!

SHANNON: Holy smoke. . . .

MAXINE: I can't quite realize it yet. . . .

SHANNON: You don't seem—inconsolable about it.

MAXINE: Fred was an old man, baby. Ten years older'n me. We hadn't had sex together in. . . .

SHANNON: What's that got to do with it?

MAXINE: Lie down and have a rum-coco.

SHANNON: No, no. I want a cold beer. If I start drinking rum-cocos now I won't stop drinking rum-cocos. So Fred is dead? I looked forward to lying in this hammock and talking to Fred.

MAXINE: Well Fred's not talking now, Shannon. A diabetic gets a blood infection, he goes like that without a decent hospital in less'n a week. [*A bus horn is heard blowing from below.*] Why don't your busload of women come on up here? They're blowing the bus horn down there.

SHANNON: Let 'em blow it, blow it. . . . [*He sways a little.*] I got a fever. [*He goes to the top of the path, divides the flowering bushes, and shouts down the hill to the bus.*] Hank! Hank! Get them out of the bus and bring 'em up here! Tell 'em the rates are OK. Tell 'em the. . . . [*His voice gives out, and he stumbles back to the verandah, where he sinks down onto the low steps, panting.*] Absolutely the worst party I've ever been out with in ten years of conducting tours. For God's sake, help me with 'em because I can't go on. I got to rest here a while. [*She gives him a cold beer.*] Thanks. Look and see if they're getting out of the

bus. [*She crosses to the masking foliage and separates it to look down the hill.*]
Are they getting out of the bus or are they staying in it, the
stingy—daughters of—bitches. . . . Schoolteachers at a Baptist
Female College in Blowing Rock, Texas. Eleven, eleven of them.

MAXINE: A football squad of old maids.

SHANNON: Yeah, and I'm the football. Are they out of the bus?

MAXINE: One's gotten out—she's going into the bushes.

SHANNON: Well, I've got the ignition key to the bus in my
pocket—this pocket—so they can't continue without me unless
they walk.

MAXINE: They're still blowin' that horn.

SHANNON: Fantastic. I can't lose this party. Blake Tours has put
me on probation because I had a bad party last month that tried to
get me sacked and I am now on probation with Blake Tours. If I
lose this party I'll be sacked for sure . . . Ah, my God, are they still
all in the bus? [*He heaves himself off the steps and staggers back to the
path, dividing the foliage to look down it, then shouts.*] Hank! Get them
out of the busssss! Bring them up heeee-re!

HANK'S VOICE [*from below*]: They wanta go back in toooooo-
wwww-n.

SHANNON: They *can't* go back in toooowwwwn!—Whew—Five
years ago this summer I was conducting round-the-world tours
for Cook's. Exclusive groups of retired Wall Street financiers. We
traveled in fleets of Pierce Arrows and Hispano Suizas.—Are they
getting out of the bus?

MAXINE: You're going to pieces, are you?

SHANNON: No! Gone! Gone! [*He rises and shouts down the hill again.*]
Hank! come up here! Come on up here a minute! I wanta talk to

you about this situation!—Incredible, fantastic . . . [*He drops back on the steps, his head falling into his hands.*]

MAXINE: They're not getting out of the bus.—Shannon . . . you're not in a nervous condition to cope with this party, Shannon, so let them go and you stay.

SHANNON: You know my situation: I lose this job, what's next? There's nothing lower than Blake Tours, Maxine honey.—Are they getting out of the bus? Are they getting out of it now?

MAXINE: Man's comin' up the hill.

SHANNON: Aw. Hank. You gotta help me with him.

MAXINE: I'll give him a rum-coco.

[HANK *comes grinning onto the verandah.*]

HANK: Shannon, them ladies are not gonna come up here, so you better come on back to the bus.

SHANNON: Fantastic.—I'm not going down to the bus and I've got the ignition key to the bus in my pocket. It's going to stay in my pocket for the next three days.

HANK: You can't get away with that, Shannon. Hell, they'll walk back to town if you don't give up the bus key.

SHANNON: They'd drop like flies from sunstrokes on that road. . . . Fantastic, absolutely fantastic . . . [*Panting and sweating, he drops a hand on* HANK'S *shoulder.*] Hank, I want your co-operation. Can I have it? Because when you're out with a difficult party like this, the tour conductor—me—and the guide—you—have got to stick together to control the situations as they come up against us. It's a test of strength between two men, in this case, and a busload of old wet *hens*! You know that, don't you?

HANK: Well. . . . [*He chuckles.*] There's this kid that's crying on the back seat all the time, and that's what's rucked up the deal. Hell, I don't know if you did or you didn't, but they all think that you did 'cause the kid keeps crying.

SHANNON: *Hank? Look!* I don't care what they think. A tour conducted by T. Lawrence Shannon is in his charge, completely— where to go, when to go, every detail of it. Otherwise I resign. So go on back down there and get them out of that bus before they suffocate in it. Haul them out by force if necessary and herd them up here. Hear me? Don't give me any argument about it. Mrs. Faulk, honey? Give him a menu, give him one of your sample menus to show the ladies. She's got a Chinaman cook here, you won't believe the menu. The cook's from Shanghai, handled the kitchen at an exclusive club there. I got him here for her, and he's a bug, a fanatic about—whew!—continental cuisine . . . can even make beef Stroganoff and thermidor dishes. Mrs. Faulk, honey? Hand him one of those—whew!—one of those fantastic sample menus. [MAXINE *chuckles, as if perpetrating a practical joke, as she hands him a sheet of paper.*] Thanks. Now, here. Go on back down there and show them this fantastic menu. Describe the view from the hill, and . . . [HANK *accepts the menu with a chuckling shake of the head.*] And have a cold Carta Blanca and. . . .

HANK: You better go down with me.

SHANNON: I can't leave this verandah for at least forty-eight hours. *What in the blazes is this?* A little animated cartoon by Hieronymus Bosch?

[*The German family which is staying at the hotel, the* FAHRENKOPFS, *their daughter and son-in-law, suddenly make a startling, dreamlike entrance upon the scene. They troop around the verandah, then turn down into the jungle path. They are all dressed in the minimal conces-*

*sion to decency and all are pink and gold like baroque cupids in various
sizes—Rubenesque, splendidly physical. The bride, HILDA, walks
astride a big inflated rubber horse which has an ecstatic smile and great
winking eyes. She shouts* "Horsey, horsey, giddap!" *as she waddles
astride it, followed by her Wagnerian-tenor bridegroom, WOLFGANG,
and her father, HERR FAHRENKOPF, a tank manufacturer from
Frankfurt. He is carrying a portable shortwave radio, which is tuned in
to the crackle and guttural voices of a German broadcast reporting the
Battle of Britain. FRAU FAHRENKOPF, bursting with rich, healthy
fat and carrying a basket of food for a picnic at the beach, brings up the
rear. They begin to sing a Nazi marching song.*]

SHANNON: Aw—Nazis. How come there's so many of them
down here lately?

MAXINE: Mexico's the front door to South America—and the
back door to the States, that's why.

SHANNON: Aw, and you're setting yourself up here as a receptionist at both doors, now that Fred's dead? [MAXINE *comes over and sits
down on him in the hammock.*] Get off my pelvis before you crack it.
If you want to crack something, crack some ice for my forehead.
[*She removes a chunk of ice from her glass and massages his forehead with
it.*]—Ah, God. . . .

MAXINE [*chuckling*]: Ha, so you took the young chick and the old
hens are squawking about it, Shannon?

SHANNON: The kid asked for it, no kidding, but she's seventeen—
less, a month less'n seventeen. So it's serious, it's very serious,
because the kid is not just emotionally precocious, she's a musical
prodigy, too.

MAXINE: What's that got to do with it?

SHANNON: Here's what it's got to do with it, she's traveling under the wing, the military escort, of this, this—butch vocal teacher who organizes little community sings in the bus. Ah, God! I'm surprised they're not singing now, they must've already suffocated. Or they'd be singing some morale-boosting number like "She's a Jolly Good Fellow" or "Pop Goes the Weasel."—Oh God. . . . [MAXINE *chuckles up and down the scale.*] And each night after supper, after the complaints about the supper and the check-up on the checks by the math instructor, and the vomiting of the supper by several ladies, who have inspected the kitchen—then the kid, the canary, will give a vocal recital. She opens her mouth and out flies Carrie Jacobs Bond or Ethelbert Nevin. I mean after a day of one indescribable torment after another, such as three blowouts, and a leaking radiator in Tierra Caliente. . . . [*He sits up slowly in the hammock as these recollections gather force.*] And an evening climb up sierras, through torrents of rain, around hairpin turns over gorges and chasms measureless to man, and with a thermos-jug under the driver's seat which the Baptist College ladies think is filled with icewater but which I know is filled with iced tequila—I mean after such a day has finally come to a close, the musical prodigy, Miss Charlotte Goodall, right after supper, before there's a chance to escape, will give a heartbreaking and earsplitting rendition of Carrie Jacobs Bond's "End of a Perfect Day"—with absolutely no humor. . . .

MAXINE: Hah!

SHANNON: Yeah, "Hah!" Last night—no, night before last, the bus burned out its brake linings in Chilpancingo. This town has a hotel . . . this hotel has a piano, which hasn't been tuned since they shot Maximilian. This Texas songbird opens her mouth and out flies "I Love You Truly," and it flies straight at *me*, with *gestures*, all right at *me*, till her chaperone, this Diesel-driven vocal instructor of hers, slams the piano lid down and hauls her out of the mess hall. But as she's hauled out Miss Bird-Girl opens her mouth and out flies, "Larry, Larry, I love you, I love you truly!" That night, when I went to my room, I found that I had a roommate.

MAXINE: The musical prodigy had moved in with you?

SHANNON: The *spook* had moved in with me. In that hot room with one bed, the width of an ironing board and about as hard, the spook was up there on it, sweating, stinking, grinning up at me.

MAXINE: Aw, the spook. [*She chuckles.*] So you've got the spook with you again.

SHANNON: That's right, he's the only passenger that got off the bus with me, honey.

MAXINE: Is he here now?

SHANNON: Not far.

MAXINE: On the verandah?

SHANNON: He might be on the other side of the verandah. Oh, he's around somewhere, but he's like the Sioux Indians in the Wild West fiction, he doesn't attack before sundown, he's an after-sundown shadow. . . .

[SHANNON *wriggles out of the hammock as the bus horn gives one last, long protesting blast.*]

MAXINE:

> I have a little shadow
> That goes in and out with me,
> And what can be the use of him
> Is more than I can see.

He's very, very like me,
From his heels up to his head,
And he always hops before me
When I hop into my bed.

SHANNON: That's the truth. He sure hops in the bed with me.

MAXINE: When you're sleeping alone, or . . . ?

SHANNON: I haven't slept in three nights.

MAXINE: Aw, you will tonight, baby.

[*The bus horn sounds again.* SHANNON *rises and squints down the hill at the bus.*]

SHANNON: How long's it take to sweat the faculty of a Baptist Female College out of a bus that's parked in the sun when it's a hundred degrees in the shade?

MAXINE: They're staggering out of it now.

SHANNON: Yeah, I've won *this* round, I reckon. What're they doing down there, can you see?

MAXINE: They're crowding around your pal Hank.

SHANNON: Tearing him to pieces?

MAXINE: One of them's slapped him, he's ducked back into the bus, and she is starting up here.

SHANNON: Oh, Great Caesar's ghost, it's the butch vocal teacher.

MISS FELLOWES [*in a strident voice, from below*]: Shannon! Shannon!

SHANNON: For God's sake, help me with her.

MAXINE: You know I'll help you, baby, but why don't you lay off the young ones and cultivate an interest in normal grown-up women?

MISS FELLOWES [*her voice coming nearer*]: Shannon!

SHANNON [*shouting down the hill*]: Come on up, Miss Fellowes, everything's fixed. [*to* MAXINE] Oh, God, here she comes chargin' up the hill like a bull elephant on a rampage!

[MISS FELLOWES *thrashes through the foliage at the top of the jungle path.*]

SHANNON: Miss Fellowes, never do that! Not at high noon in a tropical country in summer. Never charge up a hill like you were leading a troop of cavalry attacking an almost impregnable. . . .

MISS FELLOWES [*panting and furious*]: I don't want advice or instructions, I want the *bus key*!

SHANNON: Mrs. Faulk, this is Miss Judith Fellowes.

MISS FELLOWES: Is this man making a deal with you?

MAXINE: I don't know what you—

MISS FELLOWES: Is this man getting a *kickback* out of you?

MAXINE: Nobody gets any kickback out of me. I turn away more people than—

MISS FELLOWES [*cutting in*]: This isn't the Ambos Mundos. It says in the brochure that in Puerto Barrio we stay at the Ambos Mundos in the heart of the city.

SHANNON: Yes, on the plaza—tell her about the plaza.

MAXINE: What about the plaza?

SHANNON: It's hot, noisy, stinking, swarming with flies. Pariah dogs dying in the—

MISS FELLOWES: How is this place better?

SHANNON: The view from this verandah is equal and I think better than the view from Victoria Peak in Hong Kong, the view from the roof-terrace of the Sultan's palace in—

MISS FELLOWES [*cutting in*]: I want the view of a clean bed, a bathroom with plumbing that works, and food that is eatable and digestible and not contaminated by filthy—

SHANNON: *Miss Fellowes!*

MISS FELLOWES: Take your hand off my arm.

SHANNON: Look at this sample menu. The cook is a Chinese imported from Shanghai by *me*! Sent here by *me*, year before last, in nineteen thirty-eight. He was the chef at the Royal Colonial Club in—

MISS FELLOWES [*cutting in*]: You got a telephone here?

MAXINE: Sure, in the office.

MISS FELLOWES: I want to use it—I'll call collect. Where's the office.

MAXINE [*to* PANCHO]: Llévala al teléfono!

[*With* PANCHO *showing her the way,* MISS FELLOWES *stalks off around the verandah to the office.* SHANNON *falls back, sighing desperately, against the verandah wall.*]

MALCOLM LOWRY

(1909–57)

British writer Malcolm Lowry is best known for his 1947 novel, *Under the Volcano*, which is set in Quauhnahuac, Mexico, in the shadows of two volcanoes. Biographers have suggested that this tale of exile, despair, and alcoholism is highly autobiographical. In 1936, Lowry visited Mexico and lived in Cuernavaca with his first wife, Jan Gabrial. Like his protagonist Geoffrey Firmin, Lowry was an alcoholic and sought peace in exile, living in the United States, British Columbia, and Mexico.

Under the Volcano is a love story about an English consul who is losing his post and losing his wife. Alcohol is his escape and his solace and the cause of much of his pain. Much of the novel is written in stream-of-consciousness style, which blurs the edges of longing, shame, and alcohol-induced dementia. The characters find Mexico to be the perfect place both to fall in love and to suffer from its pains—"the eternal sorrow that never sleeps of great Mexico." *Under the Volcano* was made into a film, directed by John Huston, in 1984.

. . . . . . Night: and once again, the nightly grapple with death, the room shaking with daemonic orchestras, the snatches of fearful sleep, the voices outside the window, my name being continually repeated with scorn by imaginary parties arriving, the dark's spinets. As if there were not enough real noises in these nights the color of grey hair. Not like the rending tumult of American cities, the noise of the unbandaging of great giants in agony. But the howling pariah dogs, the cocks that herald dawn all night, the drumming, the moaning that will be found later white plumage huddled on telegraph wires in back gardens or fowl roosting in apple trees, the eternal sorrow that never sleeps of great Mexico. For myself I like to take my sorrow into the shadow of old monasteries, my guilt into cloisters and under tapestries, and into the misericordes of unimaginable cantinas where sad-faced potters and legless beggars drink at dawn, whose cold jonquil beauty one rediscovers in death. So that when you left, Yvonne, I went to Oaxaca. There is no sadder word. Shall I tell you, Yvonne, of the terrible journey there through the desert over the narrow gauge railway on the rack of a third-class carriage bench, the child whose life its mother and I saved by rubbing its belly with tequila out of my bottle, or of how, when I went to my room in the hotel where we once were happy, the noise of slaughtering below in the kitchen drove me out into the glare of the street, and later, that night, there was a vulture sitting in the washbasin? Horrors portioned to a giant nerve! No, my secrets are of the grave and must be kept. And this is how I sometimes think of myself, as a great explorer who has discovered some extraordinary land from which he can never return to give his knowledge to the world: but the name of this land is hell.

It is not Mexico of course but in the heart. And to-day I was in Quauhnahuac as usual when I received from my lawyer news of our divorce. This was as I invited it. I received other news too: England is breaking off diplomatic relations with Mexico and all her Consuls—those, that is, who are English—are being called home. These are kindly and good men, for the most part, whose name I suppose I demean. I shall not go home with them. I shall perhaps go home but not to England, not to that home. So, at midnight, I drove in the Plymouth to Tomalín to see my Tlaxcaltecan friend Cervantes the cockfighter at the Salón Ofélia. And thence I came to the Farolito in Parián where I sit now in a little room off the bar at four-thirty in the morning drinking ochas and then mescal and writing this on some Bella Vista notepaper I filched the other night, perhaps because the writing paper at the Consulate, which is a tomb, hurts me to look at. I think I know a good deal about physical suffering. But this is worst of all, to feel your soul dying. I wonder if it is because to-night my soul has really died that I feel at the moment something like peace.

Or is it because right through hell there is a path, as Blake well knew, and though I may not take it, sometimes lately in dreams I have been able to see it? And here is one strange effect my lawyer's news has had upon me. I seem to see now, between mescals, this path, and beyond it strange vistas, like visions of a new life together we might somewhere lead. I seem to see us living in some northern country, of mountains and hills and blue water; our house is built on an inlet and one evening we are standing, happy in one another, on the balcony of this house, looking over the water. There are sawmills half hidden by trees beyond and under the hills on the other side of the inlet, what looks like an oil refinery, only softened and rendered beautiful by distance.

It is a light blue moonless summer evening, but late, perhaps ten o'clock, with Venus burning hard in daylight, so we are certainly somewhere far north, and standing on this balcony, when from beyond along the coast comes the gathering thunder of a long many-engined freight train, thunder because though we are separated by this wide strip of water from it, the train is rolling eastward and the changing wind veers for the moment from an easterly quarter, and we face east, like Swedenborg's angels, under a sky clear save where far to the northeast over distant mountains whose purple has faded, lies a mass of almost pure white clouds, suddenly, as by a light in an alabaster lamp, illumined from within by gold lightning, yet you can hear no thunder, only the roar of the great train with its engines and its wide shunting echoes as it advances from the hills into the mountains: and then all at once a fishing boat with tall gear comes running round the point like a white giraffe, very swift and stately, leaving directly behind it a long silver scalloped rim of wake, not visibly moving inshore, but now stealing ponderously beachward toward us, this scrolled silver rim of wash striking the shore first in the distance, then spreading all along the curve of beach, its growing thunder and commotion now joined to the diminishing thunder of the train, and now breaking reboant on our beach, while the floats, for there are timber diving floats, are swayed together, everything jostled and beautifully ruffled and stirred and tormented in this rolling sleeked silver, then little by little calm again, and you see the reflection of the remote white thunderclouds in the water, and now the lightning within the white clouds in deep water, as the fishing-boat itself with a golden scroll of travelling light in its silver wake beside it reflected from the cabin vanishes round the headland, silence, and then again, within the white white distant alabaster thunderclouds beyond the mountains, the thunderless gold lightning in the blue evening, unearthly . . .

And as we stand looking all at once comes the wash of another unseen ship, like a great wheel, the vast spokes of the wheel whirling across the bay—

(Several mescals later.) Since December, 1937, and you went, and it is now I hear the spring of 1938, I have been deliberately struggling against my love for you. I dared not submit to it. I have grasped at every root and branch which would help me across this abyss in my life by myself but I can deceive myself no longer. If I am to survive I need your help. Otherwise, sooner or later, I shall fall. Ah, if only you had given me something in memory to hate you for so finally no kind thought of you would ever touch me in this terrible place where I am! But instead you sent me those letters. Why did you send the first ones to Wells Fargo in Mexico City, by the way? Can it be you didn't realise I was still here? Or— if in Oaxaca—that Quauhnahuac was still my base. That is very peculiar. It would have been so easy to find out too. And if you'd only written me *right away* also, it might have been different—sent

me a postcard even, out of the common anguish of our separation, appealing simply to *us*, in spite of all, to end the absurdity
immediately—somehow, anyhow—and saying we loved each other,
something, or a telegram, simple. But you waited too long—or so
it seems now, till after Christmas—Christmas!—and the New
Year, and then what you sent I couldn't read. No: I have scarcely
been once free enough from torment or sufficiently sober to
apprehend more than the governing design of any of these letters. But I could, can feel them. I think I have some of them on
me. But they are too painful to read, they seem too long digested.
I shall not attempt it now. I cannot read them. They break my
heart. And they came too late anyway. And now I suppose there
will be no more.

Alas, but why have I not pretended at least that I had read them,
accepted some meed of retraction in the fact that they were sent?
And why did I not send a telegram or some word immediately?
Ah, why not, why not, why not? For I suppose you would have
come back in due course if I had asked you. But this is what it is
to live in hell. I could not, cannot ask you. I could not, cannot
send a telegram. I have stood here, and in Mexico City, in the
Compañia Telegráfica Mexicana, and in Oaxaca, trembling and
sweltering in the post office and writing telegrams all afternoon,
when I had drunk enough to steady my hand, without having sent
one. And I once had some number of yours and actually called
you long distance to Los Angeles though without success. And
another time the telephone broke down. Then why do I not come
to America myself? I am too ill to arrange about the tickets, to suffer the shaking delirium of the endless weary cactus plains. And
why go to America to die? Perhaps I would not mind being buried
in the United States. But I think I would prefer to die in Mexico.

JACK KEROUAC

(1922–69)

Jack Kerouac is the best-known writer of the Beat Generation, a term he coined to describe a social and literary movement that openly defied the conservative atmosphere of the 1950s. He took several cross-country trips with his friend Neal Cassady, and the result was his novel *On the Road* (1957), which elevated him to cult status.

Kerouac used the term "fellaheen" to describe himself and his fellow Beats. This Arabic word for peasantry referred to the poor and the powerless, and these were the people Kerouac was attracted to on his journeys and wrote about in his books. He came from a Catholic home and took up the practice of Buddhism; much of his "spontaneous prose" spiritualizes experiences he has while traveling, whether friendships made or drugs tried. He visited Mexico—a place where William Burroughs spent part of his life and where Neal Cassady died prematurely—seeking friends among the "Mexico Fellaheen."

To explain, I'd missed the ship in San Pedro and this was the midway point of the trip from the Mexican border at Nogales, Arizona, that I had undertaken on cheap second-class buses all the way down the West Coast to Mexico City.—I'd met Enrique and his kid brother Gerardo while the passengers were stretching their legs at desert huts in the Sonora desert where big fat Indian ladies served hot tortillas and meat off stone stoves and as you stood there waiting for your sandwich the little pigs grazed lovingly against your legs.—Enrique was a great sweet kid with black hair and black eyes who was making this epic journey all the way to

Vera Cruz two thousand miles away on the Gulf of Mexico with his kid brother for some reason I never found out—all he let me know was that inside his home made wooden radio set was hidden about a half a pound of strong dark green marijuana with the moss still in it and long black hairs in it, the sign of good pot.— We immediately started blasting among the cacti in the back of the desert waystations, squatting there in the hot sun laughing, as Gerardo watched (he was only 18 and wasn't allowed to smoke by his older brother)—"Is why? because marijuana is bad for the eye and bad for *la ley*" (bad for the eyesight and bad for the law)— "But jew!" pointing at me (Mexican saying "you"), "and *me!*" pointing at himself, "we alright." He undertook to be my guide in the great trip through the continental spaces of Mexico—he spoke some English and tried to explain to me the epic grandeur of his land and I certainly agreed with him.—"See?" he'd say pointing at distant mountain ranges. "*Mehico!*"

The bus was an old high thin affair with wooden benches, as I say, and passengers in shawls and straw hats got on with their goats or pigs or chickens while kids rode on the roof or hung on singing and screaming from the tailgate.—We bounced and bounced over that one thousand mile dirt road and when we came to rivers the driver just plowed through the shallow water, washing off the dust, and bounced on.—Strange towns like Navajoa where I took a walk by myself and saw, in the market outdoor affair, a butcher standing in front of a pile of lousy beef for sale, flies swarming all over it while mangy skinny fellaheen dogs scrounged around under the table—and towns like Los Mochis (The Flies) where we sat drinking Orange Crush like grandees at sticky little tables, where the day's headline in the Los Mochis newspaper told of a midnight gun duel between the Chief of Police and the Mayor—it was all over town, some excitement in the white alleys—both of them with revolvers on their hips, bang, blam, right in the muddy street outside the cantina.—Now we

were in a town further south in Sinaloa and had gotten off the old
bus at midnight to walk single file through the slums and past the
bars ("Ees no good you and me and Gerardo go into cantina, ees
bad for *la ley*" said Enrique) and then, Gerardo carrying my
seabag on his back like a true friend and brother, we crossed a
great empty plaza of dirt and came to a bunch of stick huts form-
ing a little village not far from the soft starlit surf, and there we
knocked on the door of that mustachio'd wild man with the
opium and were admitted to his candlelit kitchen where he and his
witchdoctor goatee Estrando were sprinkling red pinches of pure
opium into huge cigarettes of marijuana the size of a cigar.

The host allowed us to sleep the night in the little grass hut
nearby—this hermitage belonged to Estrando, who was very kind
to let us sleep there—he showed us in by candlelight, removed his
only belongings which consisted of his opium stash under the pal-
let on the sod where he slept, and crept off to sleep somewhere
else.—We had only one blanket and tossed to see who would have
to sleep in the middle: it was the kid Gerardo, who didn't complain.—In the morning I got up and peeked out through the
sticks: it was a drowsy sweet little grass hut village with lovely
brown maids carrying jugs of water from the main well on their
shoulders—smoke of tortillas rose among the trees—dogs
barked, children played, and as I say our host was up and splitting
twigs with a spear by throwing the spear to the ground neatly part-
ing the twigs (or thin boughs) clean in half, an amazing sight.—
And when I wanted to go to the john I was directed to an ancient
stone seat which overlorded the entire village like some king's
throne and there I had to sit in full sight of everybody, it was completely in the open—mothers passing by smiled politely, children
stared with fingers in mouth, young girls hummed at their work.

We began packing to get back on the bus and carry on to Mexico City but first I bought a quarter pound of marijuana but as

soon as the deal was done in the hut a file of Mexican soldiers and a few seedy policemen came in with sad eyes.—I said to Enrique: "Hey, are we going to be arrested?" He said no, they just wanted some of the marijuana for themselves, free, and would let us go peaceably.—So Enrique cut them into about half of what we had and they squatted all around the hut and rolled joints on the ground.—I was so sick on an opium hangover I lay there staring at everybody feeling like I was about to be skewered, have my arms cut off, hung upsidedown on the cross and burned at the stake on that high stone john.—Boys brought me soup with hot peppers in it and everybody smiled as I sipped it, lying on my side—it burned into my throat, made me gasp, cough and sneeze, and instantly I felt better.

We got up and Gerardo again heaved my seabag to his back, Enrique hid the marijuana in his wooden radio, we shook hands with our host and the witchdoctor solemnly, shook hands seriously and solemnly with every one of the ten policemen and cop soldiers and off we went single file again in the hot sun towards the bus station in town.—"Now," said Enrique patting the home made radio, "see, *mir*, we all set to get high."

The sun was very hot and we were sweating—we came to a large beautiful church in the old Spanish Mission style and Enrique said: "We go in here now"—it amazed me to remember that we were all Catholics.—We went inside and Gerardo kneeled first, then Enrique and I kneed the pews and did the sign of the cross and he whispered in my ear "See? is cool in the chorch. Is good to get away from the sun a *minuto*."

At Mazatlan at dusk we stopped for awhile for a swim in our underwear in that magnificent surf and it was there, on the beach, with a big joint smoking in his hand where Enrique turned and pointed inland at the beautiful green fields of Mexico and said "See the three girls in the middle of the field far away?" and I looked and looked and only barely saw three dots in the middle of a distant pasture. "Three muchachas," said Enrique. "Is mean: *Mehico!*"

He wanted me to go to Vera Cruz with him. "I am a shoemaker by trade. You stay home with the gurls while I work, *mir?* You write you *interessa* books and we get lots of gurls."

I never saw him after Mexico City because I had no money absolutely and I had to stay on William Seward Burroughs' couch. And Burroughs didn't want Enrique around: "You shouldn't hang around with these Mexicans, they're all a bunch of con men."

I still have the rabbit's foot Enrique gave me when he left.

WILLIAM S. BURROUGHS

(1914–97)

William Burroughs had a comfortable childhood and graduated from Harvard College. After moving to New York City, Burroughs befriended Allen Ginsberg and Jack Kerouac and became part of the circle of experimental writers known as the Beats. Burroughs developed a heroin addiction, and his use of drugs came to define much of his life and work. He and his wife left New York City for East Texas and then New Orleans. Their lives there are depicted in Jack Kerouac's famous book, *On the Road*. After being arrested for drug possession, Burroughs decided not to stand trial and moved his family to Mexico City. His first novel, *Junky* (1953), originally published under a pseudonym, tells of his fifteen years as a heroin addict. His second published novel, *Naked Lunch* (1959), is a surreal ride through drugs, sex, and nightmares, and made him a countercultural icon.

The Harrison Act of 1922 outlawed narcotics and criminalized addicts and physicians who tried to treat them. Rather than being seen as "patients" as they once had been, they were labeled "dope fiends" and considered a threat to society. Subsequently, many drug users and people escaping drug charges moved from the United States to Mexico. In this excerpt from Burroughs's first novel, we see that even junkies have a saint in Mexico.

There is only one pusher in Mexico City, and that is Lupita. She has been in the business twenty years. Lupita got her start with one gram of junk and built up from there to a monopoly of the junk business in Mexico City. She weighed three hundred pounds, so she started using junk to reduce, but only her face got thin and the result is no improvement. Every month or so she hires a new lover, gives him shirts and suits and wrist watches, and then packs him in when she has enough.

Lupita pays off to operate wide open, as if she was running a grocery store. She doesn't have to worry about stool pigeons because every law in the Federal District knows that Lupita sells junk. She keeps outfits in glasses of alcohol so the junkies can fix in the joint and walk out clean. Whenever a law needs money for a quick beer, he goes over by Lupita and waits for someone to walk out on the chance he may be holding a paper. For ten pesos ($1.25) the cop lets him go. For twenty pesos, he gets his junk back. Now and then, some ill-advised citizen starts pushing better papers for less money, but he doesn't push long. Lupita has a standing offer: ten free papers to anybody who tells her about another pusher in the Federal District. Then Lupita calls one of her friends on the narcotics squad and the pusher is busted.

Lupita fences on the side. If anyone makes a good score, she puts out a grapevine to find out who was in on the job. Thieves sell to her at her price or she tips the law. Lupita knows everything that happens in the lower-bracket underworld of Mexico City. She sits there doling out papers like an Aztec goddess.

Lupita sells her stuff in papers. It is supposed to be heroin. Actually, it is pantopon cut with milk sugar and some other crap that looks like sand and remains undissolved in the spoon after you cook up.

I started scoring for Lupita's papers through Ike, the old-time junky I met in the lawyer's office. I had been off junk three months at this time. It took me just three days to get back on.

An addict may be ten years off the junk, but he can get a new habit in less than a week; whereas someone who has never been addicted would have to take two shots a day for two months to get any habit at all. I took a shot daily for four months before I could notice withdrawal symptoms. You can list the symptoms of junk sickness, but the feel of it is like no other feeling and you can not put it into words. I did not experience this junk sick feeling until my second habit.

Why does an addict get a new habit so muck quicker than a junk virgin, even after the addict has been clean for years? I do not accept the theory that junk is lurking in the body all that time— the spine is where it supposedly holes up—and I disagree with all psychological answers. I think the use of junk causes permanent cellular alteration. Once a junky, always a junky. You can stop using junk, but you are never off after the first habit.

When my wife saw I was getting the habit again, she did something she had never done before. I was cooking up a shot two days after I'd connected with Old Ike. My wife grabbed the spoon and threw the junk on the floor. I slapped her twice across the face and she threw herself on the bed, sobbing, then turned around and said to me: "Don't you want to do anything at all? You know how bored you get when you have a habit. It's like all the lights went out. Oh well, do what you want. I guess you have some stashed, anyway."

I did have some stashed.

Lupita's papers cost fifteen pesos each—about two dollars. They are half the strength of a two-dollar Stateside cap. If you have any habit at all, it takes two papers to fix you, and I mean just fix. To get really loaded, you would need four papers. I thought this was an outrageous price considering everything is cheaper in Mexico and I was expecting bargain prices on junk. And here I was, paying above-U.S. prices for junk of lower quality. Ike told me, "She has to charge high because she pays off to the law."

So I asked Ike, "What about scripts?"

He told me the croakers could only prescribe M in solution. The most they were allowed to prescribe in one script was fifteen centogramos, or about two and a half grains. I figured it would work out a lot cheaper than Lupita, so we started hitting the croakers. We located several who would write the script for five pesos, and five more who would get it filled.

One script will last a day if you keep the habit down. The trouble is, scripts are easier to get than to fill, and when you do find a drugstore that will fill the script, like as not the druggist steals all the junk and gives you distilled water. Or he doesn't have any M and puts anything on the shelf in the bottle. I have cashed scripts that came back full of undissolved powder. I could have killed myself trying to shoot this crap.

Mexican croakers are not like Stateside croakers. They never pull that professional man act on you. A croaker who will write at all will write without hearing a story. In Mexico City, there are so many doctors that a lot of them have a hard time making it. I know croakers who would starve to death if they didn't write morphine scripts. They don't have patient one, unless you call junkies patients.

I was keeping up Ike's habit as well as my own and it ran into money.

I asked Ike what the score was on pushing in Mexico City. He said it was impossible.

"You wouldn't last a week. Sure, you can get plenty customers that would pay you fifteen pesos for a shot of good M like we get with the scripts. But first time they wake up sick with no money, they go right to Lupita and tell her for a few papers. Or if the law grabs them, they open their mouth right away. Some of them don't even have to be asked. Right away they say, 'Turn me loose and I'll tell you somebody pushing junk.' So the law sends them up to make a buy with the marked money, and that's it. You're fucked right there. It's eight years for selling this stuff and there's no bail.

"I have 'em come to me: 'Ike, we know you get stuff on the scripts. Here's fifty pesos. Get me one script.' Sometimes they got good watches or a suit of clothes. I tell 'em I'm off. Sure, I could make two hundred pesos a day, but I wouldn't last a week."

"But can't you find like five or six good customers?"

"I know every hip in Mexico City. And I wouldn't trust one of 'em. Not one."

At first we filled the scripts without too much trouble. But after a few weeks the scripts had piled up in the drugstores that would fill M scripts and they began packing in. It looked like we would be back with Lupita. Once or twice we got caught short and had to score with Lupita. Using that good drugstore M had run up our habits, and it took two of Lupita's fifteen-peso papers to fix us. Now, thirty pesos in one shot was a lot more than I could afford to pay. I had to quit, cut down to where I could make it on two of Lupita's papers per day, or find another source of supply.

One of the script-writing doctors suggested to Ike that he apply for a government permit. Ike explained to me that the Mexican government issued permits to hips allowing them a definite quantity of morphine per month at wholesale prices. The doctor would put in an application for Ike for one hundred pesos. I said, "Go ahead and apply," and gave him the money. I did not expect the deal to go through, but it did. Ten days later, he had a government permit to buy fifteen grams of morphine every month. The permit had to be signed by his doctor and the head doctor at the Board of Health. Then he would take it to a drugstore and have it filled.

The price was about two dollars per gram. I remember the first time he filled the permit. A whole boxful of cubes of morphine. Like a junky's dream. I had never seen so much morphine before all at once. I put out the money and we split the stuff. Seven grams per month allowed me about three grains per day, which was more

than I ever had in the States. So I was supplied with plenty of junk
for a cost of thirty dollars a month as compared with about three
hundred a month in the U.S.

During this time I did not get acquainted with the other junkies in
Mexico City. Most of them make their junk money by stealing.
They are always hot. They are all pigeons. Not one of them can be
trusted with the price of a paper. No good can come from associ-
ating with these characters.

Ike didn't steal. He made out selling bracelets and medals that
looked like silver. He had to keep ahead of his customers because
this phony silver turned black in a matter of hours. Once or twice,
he was arrested and charged with fraud, but I always bought him
out. I told him to find some routine that was strictly legitimate,
and he started selling crucifixes.

Ike had been a booster in the States and claimed to have scored
for a hundred dollars a day in Chicago with a spring suitcase he'd
shoved suits into. The side of the suitcase would spring back into
place. All the money went for coke and M.

But Ike would not steal in Mexico. He said even the best thieves
spend most of their time in the joint. In Mexico, known thieves
can be sent to the Tres Marias penal colony without trial. There
are no middle-class, white-collar thieves who make good livings,
like you find in the States. There are big operators with political
connections, and there are bums who spend half their time in jail.
The big operators are usually police chiefs or other high officials.
That is the setup in Mexico, and Ike did not have connections to
operate.

One junky I did see from time to time was a dark-skinned
Yucatecan whom Ike referred to as "the Black Bastard." The
Black Bastard worked the crucifix routine. He was, in fact, ex-
tremely religious and made the pilgrimage to Chalma every year,

going the last quarter mile on his knees over rocks with two people holding him up. After that, he was fixed for a year.

Our Lady of Chalma seems to be the patron saint of junkies and cheap thieves because all Lupita's customers make the pilgrimage once a year. The Black Bastard rents a cubicle in the church and pushes papers of junk outrageously cut with milk sugar.

I used to see the Black Bastard around from time to time, and I heard a great deal about him from Ike. Ike hated the Black Bastard only as one junky can hate another. "The Black Bastard burned down that drugstore. Going up there saying I sent him. Now the druggist won't fill no more scripts."

So I drifted along from month to month. We were always a little short at the end of the month and had to fill a few scripts. I always had an insecure feeling when I was out of stuff and a comfortable feeling of security when I had those seven gramos stashed safely away.

Once Ike got fifteen days in the city prison—the Carmen, they call it—for vagrancy. I was short and could not pay the fine, and it was three days before I got in to see him. His body had shrunk; all the bones stuck out in his face; his brown eyes were bright with pain. I had a piece of hop covered with cellophane in my mouth. I spit the hop on half an orange and handed it to Ike. In twenty minutes, he was loaded.

I looked around and noticed how the hips stood out as a special group, like the fags who were posturing and screeching in one corner of the yard. The junkies were grouped together, talking and passing the junky gesture back and forth.

Junkies all wear hats, if they have hats. They all look alike, as if wearing a costume identical in some curious way that escapes exact tabulation. Junk has marked them all with its indelible brand.

Ike told me that the prisoners often steal the pants off a newcomer. "Such a lousy people they got in here." I did see several men walking around in their underwear. The Commandante would catch wives and relatives bringing junk to the prisoners, and shake them down for all they had.

He caught one woman bringing a paper to her husband, but she only had five pesos. So he took her dress and sold it for fifteen pesos and she went home wrapped in an old lousy sheet.

The place was crawling with pigeons. Ike was afraid to hold any of the hop I brought him for fear the other prisoners would take it or turn him over to the Commandante.

DONNA M. GERSHTEN

(1953–)

Donna M. Gershten was born in eastern North Carolina and later lived for some years in Sinaloa, Mexico, where she ran a fitness and community center. She was awarded the first Bellwether Prize for Fiction for her first novel, *Kissing the Virgin's Mouth*, in 2000. The Bellwether Prize was established by author Barbara Kingsolver to promote literature of "social responsibility" and "political boldness and complexity." In this debut, the narrator, Guadalupe Magdalena Molina Vásquez, who has grown up in extreme poverty in Teatlán, Sinaloa, uses her young body and sharp mind to escape and create a new life for herself.

Two nights and two days later, the bus pulled into the Tijuana station. With my bundle clutched to my chest like a schoolgirl's books, I stood from my seat, bumping the child who slept sweaty against my shoulder, squeezed through the aisle of passengers unloading their boxes, and stepped down from the bus. Without stopping to use the toilet or to ask a question, I walked. Everything in my young body urged me to move forward, to focus through and past the station chaos to a better place, to my new life.

Some streets later, my pace slowed, my focus softened and my belly spoke the truth of its emptiness. A handwritten sign advertised *comida corrida*, and I stepped into the small alcove, sat at a table and secured the bundle between my feet.

"*Buenas,*" a woman said as she bent to relight the burners beneath large metal pots.

It was late for *comida* and the tables, all but mine, were empty.

The woman soon stood over me with a plate in one hand and a tortilla basket in the other.

"*¿Comida?*" She set the plate on the sticky oilcloth before I had answered, and returned to the open corner that was the kitchen.

The last serving of the day was mounded lukewarm and over-cooked on the plate before me—*sopa seca, carne asada,* frijoles, and a basket of tortillas—and though the *sopa seca* was sticky and the meat tough, it was cheap and the first real meal I had eaten since leaving Teatlán.

"From where do you come, *hija?*" The woman reached her arm deep inside a stained and dented pot to scrape the remains of the food with her hand.

"Teatlán, Sinaloa, señora." It gave me pleasure to do something so ordinary as push a fork full of beans creamy with *manteca* against a rolled tortilla; to hear the detached and easy voice of a woman working; to hear my own lies affirmed in my own voice. I told her that I was going to be a dancer, that I would send money to my family, maybe buy them a car, have a nice place of my own.

"Already you have a job, *hija?*" she asked.

A man holding a sack of sugar on one shoulder stepped into the niche and the cook raised her chin to him in greeting. She pointed to me with her head. "A friend from Teatlán," she introduced me. "My husband." She nodded from him to me.

"Eugenio de Dios, *para servirle.*" He set the heavy sack on the floor by his wife.

I nodded and spoke with a mouth too full. "Magdalena Molina Vásquez."

The young me thought it decent that this couple would be kind to me, that they would offer to rent me a room; I thought it nice that Eugenio de Dios would insist that he accompany me to find a relatively safe job dancing at Club Leona. Remembering Tijuana with all I know now, I understand what a *verdadero milagro* it is that

I survived. A true miracle. Thank La Lupa. Thank cheap bad food. Thank *los angeles* Carmen and Eugenio de Dios.

Tijuana was filled with dancing jobs. Dancing meant many things that I had not imagined. There was dancing without clothes, dancing over the faces of drunk men who inserted cash and coins into the *cosita*. Dancing I would not perform. I learned this all after I was go-go dancing in Club Leona. Listening to the gossip of dancers and bartenders and busboys, I heard the stories: of private curtained lap-dance rooms, of a woman from Club Tigre who inserted a shot glass full of tequila into her *cosita*, danced her hip circles, then took the glass out still full and drank it; of men who squeezed *limón* halves over the *cositas* of *putas* to check for sores that would burn from the acid; of a woman who danced around the giant *chile* of a donkey; of a dancer violated by a customer on the stage while the audience applauded. Some of the dancers at Club Leona carried a potent powder to dissolve into the drinks of aggressive customers.

Pure luck, pure ignorance and grace—pure something— protected me.

Then I did not know just how grateful to be. I did not know enough to have fear.

But I knew shame. Sometimes, dancing and sweating in color and tassels through blinking lights safe in the go-go cage above the crowd in Club Leona, I would imagine my mother fingering the good-bye note slowly, pretending she could read it, moving her lips the way she did, crying, crying at her table. Chucha standing behind Mami's chair. I imagined the warm weight of Chucha's open palms pressing on the top of Mami's shoulders. I had left Teatlán knowing that I must escape, hoping I could earn more if I went to Tijuana, telling myself it was for my family too, that maybe I would earn enough to heal Mami, to buy them a house, more food. Good doctors. Lies to help me flee. I danced through the shame.

Every night I celebrated and grieved. I safely burned my soul on that platform. Dancing.

I had learned to dance on rooftops. The dance grounds were not far from our house, and with my mother and my brothers and my sisters, I would stand on our flat roof and listen to the distant music. My sister, Rosa, taught me *los pasos a seguir*. She held me in her arms and we danced, damp faces together cheek to cheek, circling the rebar, the *tejuino* pot, ducking the clothesline, until she tired from holding me and set me on my feet so that we continued to shuffle circles cheek to belly.

When I had nine years, my sister, Rosa, took me to her friend's rooftop that overlooked the dance grounds. From surrounding ranchitos and barrios, people came by bus and car and foot. To dance. Each man was given a strip of white cloth to tie on his upper arm after he paid the five centavos. Only men paid. On the rooftop, men who couldn't afford a white band, women and girls too young or shy to attend, danced, and from that roof's edge, my sister and I watched the dancers below, an ocean of cowboy hats and dark heads rocking, bobbing, spinning beneath us, couples curved and tangled, to the tuba and clarinets, the churning of the Sinaloense. So many people pressed together so tightly. They danced to the song "No Volveré," and looking down on the people, I wanted to dive from the roof like the beach boys from the cliffs over the ocean, just like them to arch my back and then point myself like an arrow into the dancers, to swim in the middle of elbows and knees, to disappear into the music.

ICONS AND IDENTITY

Patria and Pilgrims

RICHARD RODRIGUEZ

(1944-)

Richard Rodriguez has become an unofficial spokesperson for the complexities of Mexican culture in the United States. He crafts complex, provoking essays about language, religion, family, and cultural and religious icons. An editor at Pacific News Service and a contributing editor for *Harper's Magazine, U.S. News & World Report*, and the *Los Angeles Times*, Rodriguez has authored three books: *Brown: The Last Discovery of America* (2002); *Days of Obligation: An Argument with My Mexican Father* (1992); and *Hunger of Memory* (1981) as well as two BBC documentaries.

In his collection of essays *Days of Obligation*, Rodriguez moves between California and Mexico, at once debunking cultural myths and pulling together themes seemingly at odds—poverty and business opportunities in Tijuana, faith and the AIDS epidemic in San Francisco, and the Catholic Church and indigenous people in the Americas. With his unique vision and clarity, he explains the allure of the Virgin of Guadalupe and her revered stature in Mexican culture, which has been taking hold on both sides of the border.

The Virgin of Guadalupe symbolizes the entire coherence of Mexico, body and soul. You will not find the story of the Virgin within hidebound secular histories of Mexico—nor indeed within the credulous repertoire of Señor Fuentes—and the omission renders the history of Mexico incomprehensible.

One recent afternoon, within the winy bell jar of a very late lunch, I told the story of the Virgin of Guadalupe to Lynn, a sophisticated twentieth-century woman. The history of Mexico, I promised her, is neither mundane nor masculine, but it is a miracle play with trapdoors and sequins and jokes on the living.

In the sixteenth century, when Indians were demoralized by the routing of their gods, when millions of Indians were dying from the plague of Europe, the Virgin Mary appeared pacing on a hillside to an Indian peasant named Juan Diego—his Christian name, for Juan was a convert. It was December 1531.

On his way to mass, Juan passed the hill called Tepayac . . .

> *Just as the East was beginning to kindle*
> *To dawn. He heard there a cloud*
> *Of birdsong bursting overhead*
> *Of whistles and flutes and beating wings*
> *—Now here, now there—*
> *A mantle of chuckles and berries and rain*
> *That rocked through the sky like the great Spanish bell*
> *In Mexico City;*
> *At the top of the hill there shone a light*
> *And the light called out a name to him*
> *With a lady's voice.*
> *Juan, Juan,*
> *The Lady-light called.*
> *Juan crossed himself, he fell to his knees,*
> *He covered his eyes and prepared to be blinded.*
>
> *He could see through his hands that covered his face,*
> *As the sun rose up from behind her cape,*
> *That the poor light of day*
> *Was no match for this Lady, but broke upon her*
> *Like a waterfall,*
> *A rain of rings.*
> *She wore a gown the color of dawn.*
> *Her hair was braided with ribbons and flowers*

And tiny tinkling silver bells. Her mantle was sheer
And bright as rain and embroidered with thousands
of twinkling stars.
A clap before curtains, like waking from sleep;
Then a human face,
A mother's smile;
Her complexion as red as cinnamon bark;
Cheeks as brown as persimmon.

Her eyes were her voice,
As modest and shy as a pair of doves
In the eaves of her brow. Her voice was
Like listening. This lady spoke
In soft Nahuatl, the Aztec tongue
(As different from Spanish
As some other season of weather,
As doves in the boughs of a summer tree
Are different from crows in a wheeling wind,
Who scatter destruction and
Caw caw caw caw)—
Nahuatl like rain, like water flowing, like drips in a cavern,
Or glistening thaw,
Like breath through a flute,
With many stops and plops and sighs . . .

Peering through the grille of her cigarette smoke, Lynn heard and she seemed to approve the story.

At the Virgin's behest, this Prufrock Indian must go several times to the bishop of Mexico City. He must ask that a chapel be built on Tepayac where his discovered Lady may share in the sorrows of her people. Juan Diego's visits to the Spanish bishop parody the conversion of the Indians by the Spaniards. The bishop is skeptical.

The bishop wants proof.

The Virgin tells Juan Diego to climb the hill and gather a sheaf of roses as proof for the bishop—Castilian roses—impossible in Mexico in December of 1531. Juan carries the roses in the folds of his cloak, a pregnant messenger. Upon entering the bishop's presence, Juan parts his cloak, the roses tumble; the bishop falls to his knees.

In the end—with crumpled napkins, torn carbons, the bitter dregs of coffee—Lynn gave the story over to the Spaniards.

The legend concludes with a concession to humanity—proof more durable than roses—the imprint of the Virgin's image upon the cloak of Juan Diego . . .

A Spanish trick, Lynn said. A recruitment poster for the new religion, no more, she said (though sadly). An itinerant diva with a costume trunk. Birgit Nilsson as Aïda.

Why do we assume Spain made up the story?

The importance of the story is that Indians believed it. The jokes, the vaudeville, the relegation of the Spanish bishop to the role of comic adversary, the Virgin's chosen cavalier, and especially the brown-faced Mary—all elements spoke directly to Indians.

The result of the apparition and of the miraculous image of the Lady remaining upon the cloak of Juan Diego was a mass conversion of Indians to Catholicism.

The image of Our Lady of Guadalupe (privately, affectionately, Mexicans call her La Morenita—Little Darkling) has become the unofficial, the private flag of Mexicans. Unique possession of her image is a more wonderful election to Mexicans than any political call to nationhood. Perhaps Mexico's tragedy in our century, perhaps Mexico's abiding grace thus far, is that she has no political idea of herself as compelling as her icon.

The Virgin appears everywhere in Mexico. On dashboards and on calendars, on playing cards, on lampshades and cigar boxes;

within the loneliness and tattooed upon the very skins of Mexicans.

Nor is the image of Guadalupe a diminishing mirage of the sixteenth century, but she has become more vivid with time, developing in her replication from earthy shades of melon and musk to bubble-gum pink, Windex blue, to achieve the hard, literal focus of holy cards or baseball cards; of Krishna or St. Jude or the Atlanta Braves.

Mexico City stands as the last living medieval capital of the world. Mexico is the creation of a Spanish Catholicism that attempted to draw continents together as one flesh. The success of Spanish Catholicism in Mexico resulted in a kind of proof—a profound concession to humanity: the *mestizaje*.

What joke on the living? Lynn said.

The joke is that Spain arrived with missionary zeal at the shores of contemplation. But Spain had no idea of the absorbent strength of Indian spirituality.

By the waters of baptism, the active European was entirely absorbed within the contemplation of the Indian. The faith that Europe imposed in the sixteenth century was, by virtue of the Guadalupe, embraced by the Indian. Catholicism has become an Indian religion. By the twenty-first century, the locus of the Catholic Church, by virtue of numbers, will be Latin America, by which time Catholicism itself will have assumed the aspect of the Virgin of Guadalupe.

Brown skin.

ANA CASTILLO

(1953–)

Ana Castillo is the author of the novels *The Mixquiahuala Letters* (1987), *So Far From God* (1993), *Peel My Love Like an Onion* (1999), and most recently, *Watercolor Women, Opaque Men* (2005). A poet, she's known for her collections *My Father Was a Toltec* (2004) and *I Ask the Impossible* (2001). She has received numerous awards, including the American Book Award and the Carl Sandburg Award.

Born into a Mexican community in Chicago, Ana Castillo writes works that can be considered acts of translation of the intimate, religious, and economic lives of people who are often unheard in this country. Through her lyricism, their thoughts and dreams become known and their lives become a vivid reality for readers. In this personal essay, "My Mother's México," Ana Castillo writes about going back to Mexico to visit her mother's family, and the harsh reality of *vecindades*, or communal living. This essay was originally published in *Hungry Mind Review*, and recorded for National Public Radio's program *Crossroads*. Amid the poverty of Mexico City, and within the bonds of family and history, this poet finds her voice.

MY MOTHER'S MÉXICO

My mother's México was the brutal urban reality of Luis Bunuel's *Los Olvidados*. Children scamming and hustling: fire-eaters, hubcap stealers, Chiclet sellers, miniature accordion players with small, dirty hands stretched out before passersby for a coin, a piece of bread, "Please señor, for my mother who is very sick." This was the Mexico City of my family. This was the México my mother spared me.

In that Mexico City in the 1930s, Mami was a street urchin, not an orphan—not yet—with one ragged dress. Because of an unnamed skin disease that covered her whole tiny body with scabs, her head was shaved. At seven years old or maybe eight, she scurried, quick and invisible as a Mayan messenger, through the throngs of that ancient metropolis in the area known as "La Villita," where the goddess Tonantzin/Guadalupe had made her divine appearances four times and ordered el Indio Juan Diego four times to tell the Catholic officials to build Her a church. "Yes!" and off he went, sure-footed and trembling. Mami, who was not Mami but little then, bustled on her own mission toward the corner where her stepfather sold used paperbacks on the curb. At midday he ordered his main meal from a nearby restaurant and ate it out of stainless steel carryout containers without leaving his "place of business." The little girl would take the leftovers and dash them off to her mother who was lying on a *petate*—in the one room the whole family shared in a *vecindad* overflowing with families like their own with all manner of maladies that accompany destitution. Her mother was dying.

María de los Angeles Rocha de Castro spent her days and nights in the dark, windowless room reading novels—used paperbacks provided by her new husband from Vera Cruz—seconds like the food he shared with her. She copied favorite passages and verses into a notebook, which I have inherited, not through the pages of a will but by my mother's will: she carried the notebook, preserved in its faded newsprint cover, over decades of migration and one day not that long ago, handed it over to me, the daughter who also liked to read, to write, to save things.

María de los Angeles named her second daughter after a fictional character, Florinda, but my mother was the eldest daughter.

She was not named for romance like my tía Flora—aromatic and evocative—but from the Old Testament, Raquel, a name as impenetrable as the rock in her parents' shared Guanajuatan family name, Rocha: Raquel Rocha Rocha. And quite a rock my mother has been all the days of her life, Moses and Mount Sinai and God striking lightning all over the place, Raquel the Rock.

One day, María de los Angeles—the maternal grandmother whom I never knew but am so much like I'm told—asked her eldest daughter to purchase a harmonica for her. Of course it would be a cheap one that could be obtained from a street vendor not unlike her bookselling husband. This the child did and brought it to her mother's deathbed, a straw mat on a stone floor. And when the mother felt well enough, she produced music out of the little instrument, in the dark of that one room in Mexico City, the city where she had gone with her parents and two eldest children with the hope of getting good medical care that could rarely be found in those days outside the capital.

Instead, María stood in line outside a dispensary. Dispensaries were medical clinic substitutes, equipped to offer little more than drugs, certain common injections, and lightweight medical advice. In a rosary chain of women like herself—black rebozos, babies at their breast—she waited for hours in the sun or rain, on the ground, so many lives, and that woman at the end, there, yes, that one, my mother's young mother waited, dying.

In the 1970s while I was living alone in Mexico City, I had a medical student friend who took me to such a dispensary where he worked most evenings. The place, located in a poor *colonia*, consisted of two dark rooms—one for the receptionist and the other for consultation. The dispensary was crammed to the ceiling with boxes of drugs, mostly from the United States, which were administered freely to patients. I knew almost nothing about medication, but I knew that in the United States we did not have a once-a-month birth control pill, and that belladonna could not be taken without a doctor's prescription. And yet, drugs such as these were abundant in the dispensary, and my young friend, not only not a doctor but in fact failing medical school, was permitted to prescribe at his own discretion.

María de los Angeles was newly widowed during her dispensary days, and why she married again so soon (the bookseller) I cannot say, except that she was so sick with two children that shelter and leftovers may have been reason enough. She bore two children quickly from this second marriage so unlike the first in which, among other differences, it took seven years before the couple had their first child, a son born in Kansas, and two years later, a daughter, my mother, born in Nebraska.

My grandfather, my mother has often told me, worked on the railroads as a signal man. This is what brought the Guanajuatan couple to the United States. From this period—1920s—I can construct a biography of the couple myself because María de los Angeles was very fond of being photographed. She wore fine silks and chiffons and wide-brimmed hats. Her handlebar moustached husband with the heavy lidded eyes telling of his Indian ancestry, sported a gold pocket watch. They drove a Studebaker.

After the 1929 stock market crash, Mexican workers in the United States, suddenly jobless, were quickly returned to the other side of the border. My grandparents returned not with severance pay, not with silk dresses nor wool suits, not with the Studebaker—but with tuberculosis. My grandfather died soon after.

When María de los Angeles died (not surprisingly she was not saved by the rudimentary medical treatment she received at dispensaries), her children—two sons, two daughters—were sent out to work to earn their own keep. Where the sons went I don't know. But I know about the daughters—Raquel and her younger sister, Flora—because when they grew up and became women they told me, in kitchens, over meals, into late evenings, that by the time they were about ten years old they were live-in domestics.

My mother was a little servant (and that is why she now keeps a neat home). My tía Flora was sent to the kitchen of an Arab family. And although her house now is always crowded, crazy chaos, she became the best Mexican cook on both sides of the border. (That is why it's a Tenochtitlán feast at tía Flora's table in her humble casita at the outpost of Mesoamerica—that is to say, the *mero corazón* of the Mexican barrio of Chicago: spices and sauces of cumin and sesame seeds, chocolate, ground peanuts, and all varieties of chiles, cuisines far from shy or hesitant but bold and audacious, of fish, fowl, and meats, feasts fit for a queen.)

When my mother was about seventeen, her guardian grandparents decided to take their U.S.-born grandchildren closer to the border. The strategy of the migrating *abuelos* was that the U.S.-born grandchildren could get better work or, at least, perhaps better pay on the U.S. side. They settled in Nuevo Laredo. One year later my mother was either raped or at least clearly taken advantage of by the owner of the restaurant on the U.S. side of the border where she found work as a waitress. She has never said which it was. He was married with a family and considerably older than the teenager who bore his son. The best my great-grandfather could do at that point on behalf of my mother's honor was to get the man to provide for her. So he paid the rent on a little one-room wooden house, which of course gave him further claims on my mother. Two years later, a daughter was born.

Three years more and Mami's México ended as a daily construction of her reality when, with machete in hand, she went out to make her own path. She left her five-year-old son with her sister Flora, who was newly wed and soon-to-be-widowed, and with her three-year-old girl followed some cousins who had ventured even further north to find work. Six months later she returned for her son, and when the three went up north this time she would move to Chicago alone with her children. Mami remembers all this as the longest year of her life.

My mother went to work in factories where she got some benefits and bonuses on assembly lines and varicose veins and a paralyzed thumb one day when a punch press went through it. Doña Jovita, the *curandera* who took care of Mami's two children, convinced Mami to marry her teenage son. The next summer I was born. Mami stayed in factories until the last one closed up and went off to Southeast Asia, leaving its union workers without work, without pay, and some without pension, and sending Mami into early retirement.

My Mami, a dark mestiza, inherited the complexes and fears of the colonized and the strange sense of national pride that permeates the new society of the conquered. To this day, Mami speaks only Spanish, although she has lived in Chicago for over forty years. She throws out English words—zas, zas, zas, like stray bullets—at gringos, at grandchildren, at her African American Avon manager, like a misfiring pistol.

When I was twelve, I saw Mami's Mexico City for the first time. My mother and I traveled from Chicago to Nuevo Laredo by car. It was possibly the hottest place on earth in the month of July. But Mami didn't have much choice about when to travel since the first two weeks of July were when the factory where she worked closed down and workers were given vacation time. Mami paid a young Mexican who was looking for riders to take us. The car broke down, we slept in it at night, we were refused service at gas stations and in restaurants here and there in the South—in Texas I remember—and finally we got to my great-grandmother's two-room wooden house with an outhouse and a shower outside. Two years before when we visited my great-grandmother, I had made friends with the little girl next door. At that time we climbed trees and fed the chickens and took sides with each other against her older brother. That's how and why I learned to write Spanish—I wanted to write to Rosita. (My mother, after long days at the factory, would come home to make dinner, and after the dishes and just before bed, she, with her sixth grade education, would sit me down at the kitchen table and teach me how to write to Rosita in Spanish, phonetically, with soft vowels, with humor, with a pencil and no book.) But this time, Rosita was fourteen. She had crossed over to that place of no return—breasts and boys. And not long after that, Rosita ran away.

In Nuevo Laredo we were met by my tía Flora who had also traveled from Chicago—with her five children, ranging from ages fourteen to four. The husbands of these two sisters did not come along on this pilgrimage because there are men who despite having families are not family men. They passed up their traditional right to accompany their wives and children on this adventure.

There were too many children to sleep in the house, so we were sent up to the flat roof to sleep under the stars. My mother had not known that she needed permission from my father to take me into México, so with my cousin's birth certificate to pass me off as Mexican-born, we all got on a train one day, and I illegally entered Mami's Mexico City.

Our life in Chicago was not suburban backyards with swings and grassy lawn. It was not ample living rooms and your own bedroom. It was not what I saw on TV. And yet it was not the degree of poverty in which we all found ourselves immersed overnight, through inheritance, birth, the luck or bad luck, rather, of destiny. It was the destiny that my mother and her sister dodged by doing as their mother, María de los Angeles, had decades before—for a period of her life at least—by getting the hell out of México however they could. It was the destiny in México that my mother's little brother Leonel refused to reject because of his hatred for capitalism, which he felt was fully embodied by the United States.

So Leonel, dark and handsome in his youth, with thin lips that curled up giving him the permanent smiling expression of a cynic, came to get us at the little hotel in Mexico City where my mother's stepfather, who was still selling books on a street corner, had installed us the night before. He met us at the train station, feeding us all bowls of *atole* for our late meal at the restaurant where his credit was good.

My cousin Sandra and I opened the door for tío Leonel. We didn't know who he was. We told him our mothers had gone on an errand, taking the younger children with them. My tío Leonel did not step all the way into the room. We were young females alone and for him to do so would have been improper. He looked me up and down with black eyes, as black as my mother's, as black as mine, and knitted eyebrows as serious as Mami's and as serious as mine have become. "You are Raquel's daughter?" he asked. I nodded. And then he left.

He returned for us later, Mami and me and my tía Flora and her five children, eight of us altogether, plus big suitcases, and took us to his home. Home for tío Leonel was a single dark room in a *vecindad. Vecindades* are communal living quarters. Families stay in single rooms. They share toilet and water facilities. The women have a tiny closet for a kitchen just outside their family's room, and they cook on a griddle on the floor. I don't remember my uncle's common-law-wife's name. I am almost certain that it was María, but that could be a lucky guess. I remember my cousins who were all younger than me and their crazy *chilango* accents. But I don't remember their names or how many there were then. There were nearly ten—but not ten yet—because that would be the total number my uncle and his woman would eventually have. Still, it felt like ten. So now there were four adults and at least thirteen children, age fourteen and under, staying in one room.

We didn't have to worry about crowding the bathroom because the toilets were already shared by the entire *vecindad.* There were no lights and no plumbing. At night sometimes, my uncle cleverly brought in an electrical line from outside and connected a bulb.

This was not always possible or safe. The sinks used for every kind of washing were unsanitary. Sandra and I went to wash our hands and faces one morning and both stepped back at the sight of a very ugly black fish that had burst out of the drainpipe and was swimming around in the large plugged-up basin.

For entertainment we played bolero with our cousins who were experts—bolero, the handheld toy, not Ravel's music. The object of the game is to flip a wooden ball onto a peg. My little cousins could not afford a real bolero, of course, and therefore made their own, using cans, old string, and stones or cork.

A neighbor in the *vecindad* who owned the local candy stand had a black-and-white TV. At a certain hour every evening, she charged the children who wanted to, or rather, who could afford it, to sit in the store to watch their favorite cartoon show.

I was twelve, Sandra (my cousin and also my best friend) thirteen, and her brother, Eloy, fourteen. We were beyond cartoon shows and taking bolero contests seriously, and we were talking our early teen-talk to each other in English. It was 1965 and the Rolling Stones were singing "Can't Get No Satisfaction" in English over Spanish radio on my cousin's made-in-Japan transistor, and we insolent U.S.-born adolescents wanted no part of México. Not the México of the amusement park, La Montaña Rusa, where we went one day and had great fun on the roller coaster. Not the México of sleeping under the stars on the roof of my tío Aurelio's home in Nuevo Laredo. Not the México of the splendid gardens of Chapultepec Park, of the cadet heroes, Los Niños Heroes, who valiantly but fatally fought off the invasion of U.S. troops. But of a México where we all slept on the mattress our mothers had purchased for us on the first night in my tío Leonel's home. It was laid out in the middle of the room, and six children and two grown women slept on it crossways, lined up neatly like Chinese soldiers in the frontline at night in the trenches. My tío and his wife and children slept all around us on piles of rags.

We had, with one train ride, stepped right into our mothers' Mexico City, unchanged in the nearly two decades since their departure.

Then in 1976 when I was living on my own in California, I met my family at the appointed meeting place—my tío Aurelio's in Nuevo Laredo—and traveled south by van with everybody to Mexico City. My tía Flora, this time without any of her children, came along too. The great-grandmother, Apolinar, had died and we had only recently received word of it. The grand-uncle and border official, tío Aurelio, had a heart condition, and we would not see him again after this visit. My tía Flora's veracruzano book-selling father had also died that year. We had only the little brother Leonel to visit. The young anticapitalist—once so proud of his sole possession (a new bicycle, which eventually was stolen), devoted to his family in his own way (although the older children had gone off on their own, while the youngest sold Chiclets on the streets)—was on his deathbed at forty.

He was dying of corroded liver, cirrhosis-ridden. By then, his lot had improved so that he had two rooms, a real bed, and electricity, but not much more. We stood around his bed and visited awhile so he could meet his brother-in-law and some other members of my mother's family whom he had never known before.

We went to visit his oldest daughter, around my age, at the house where she worked as a live-in domestic. She could not receive company, of course, but was allowed to visit with us outside for a bit.

We went to visit her older brother, too. He had an honest-to-goodness apartment—three whole rooms and its own kitchen. He worked in a factory and had a young family of his own.

One evening my tía Flora and I ran into Leonel on the street, not far from where the cousin with the apartment lived. He was now a yellowish wire of a man and appeared quite drunk. His pants were held up by a rope. He glanced at me and then asked my tía Flora, "Is this Raquel's daughter?" My tía, in her usual happy-sounding way said, "Yes, yes, of course she is the *hija* of Raquel." And then Tía, who is more veracruzana than *chilanga*—that is, more palm than granite—laughed a summer rainstorm laugh.

Of course I was and am the daughter of Raquel. But I was the one born so far north that not only my tío but all my relatives in México found it hard to think me real. The United States was Atlantis, and there was no Atlantis; and therefore having been born there, I could not exist. He nodded at my aunt, who was real, but not at me, who was a hologram, and went on his way. "My poor brother," my tía said, "he looks like Cantinflas," comparing him to the renowned Mexican comedian, famous for his derelict appearance and street ways. That was the last we saw him, and by end of summer he had died.

If the double rock in Mami's name and the castle at the end through marriage had dubbed her the stoic sister, the flower in Flora's name perfumed her urban life and warded off the sadness of trying times. And those had been many in my tía's life, multiplied with the years as her children grew up far from México in Chicago's poverty.

So it was that night that my tía and I, riding a city bus, jumped off suddenly in a plaza where trios and duos of musicians gathered for hire, and we brought a late-night serenade to Mami and family at our hotel. That was when my tía Flora and I bonded as big-time dreamers, and it was that night, after the serenade and after Dad (who came on this trip) had brought out a bottle of mescal and we had all shared a drink with the musicians, that Mami told me some of the stories I tell you now.

By migrating Mami saved me from the life of a live-in domestic and perhaps from inescapable poverty in Mexico City. But it was the perseverance of Raquel the Rock and the irrepressible sensuality of Flora the thick-stemmed calla lily that saved me too. "Ana del Aire," my mother calls me. Woman of the air, not earth-bound, rooted to one place—not to México where Mami's mother died, not to Chicago where I was born, not to New Mexico where I've made a home for my son, but to everywhere at once.

And when the world so big becomes a small windowless room, I draw from the vision of María de los Angeles. I read and write poems. I listen to music, I sing—with the voice of my ancestors from Guanajuato who had birds in their throats. I paint with my heart, with acrylics on linen and cotton. I talk to my son, to my lover, and with my *comadres* on the telephone. I tell a story. I make a sound and leave a mark—as palatable as a prickly pear, more solid than stone.

RUBÉN MARTÍNEZ

(1962-)

Los Angeles native Rubén Martínez is an award-winning journalist, author, and musician. His books include *The New Americans* (2004); *Crossing Over: A Mexican Family on the Migrant Trail* (2001); *Eastside Stories* (with Joseph Rodriguez, 1998); and *The Other Side: Notes from the New L.A., Mexico City, and Beyond* (Vintage, 1993). His essays, opinions, and reportage have appeared in *The New York Times*, *Washington Post*, *Los Angeles Times*, and *Mother Jones*, and as a political commentator he has appeared on ABC's *Nightline*, PBS's *Frontline*, National Public Radio's *All Things Considered*, and on CNN.

The son of immigrants, Martínez was drawn to the great American epic tale of immigration—specifically the perilous and porous border between Mexico and the United States. The tragic tale of the Chávez family of Cheran, in Michoacan, Mexico, is the impetus for *Crossing Over*. Three brothers— Benjamín, Jaime, and Salvador Chávez—were on their way to their work in the strawberry fields of Watsonville, California, in 1996. While fleeing a Border Patrol vehicle, the van they were in, overloaded with illegal migrants, crashed and all three brothers were killed. Martínez follows the lives of their family and neighbors in the wake of this tragedy. In this excerpt, Martínez explains *la crisis*—the financial catastrophe in Mexico that forced thousands of people to make the illicit crossing to help their families survive.

Lent in the Year of Our Lord 1996 was, for Mexicans, the darkest hour before the dawn. Certainly they hoped it was the darkest hour. The thought that there could actually be more suffering visited upon their country was too much to bear; Mexicans always prefer to invoke the resurrection.

This was the third consecutive Lent observed in a time of crisis. Since New Year's Day 1994, the stock market had plunged alongside the peso, the jobless rate had soared, and the black market had exploded. The rich tightened their belts, the middle class strained under massive debt. For the Mexican worker or peasant, it was yet another round of survival. The streets of Mexico City were choked as never before with street vendors, prostitutes, pickpockets, and incipient youth gangs aping their counterparts in Compton and East L.A. And then there were the poorest of the poor, the Indians living in the provinces, a good many of whom had become convinced that, in the face of such adversity, revolution was the only recourse. That or crossing the border.

In the border states, narco-wars raged. Mob-style hits were carried out on the streets in broad daylight. Much of Mexican airspace was ruled by a man nicknamed El Señor de los Cielos, the Lord of the Skies, aka Amado Carrillo Fuentes, a cartel godfather who shipped his cargo, by the tons, on chartered jet planes.

Despite forecasts of better times (the Clinton administration even chipped in $50 billion in credit to prop up its free-trade partner), the darkness lingered on. Assassinations, corruption, street crime. In everyday conversation, Mexicans referred to the phenomenon as, simply, "*la crisis.*" They uttered the phrase with almost sentimental familiarity, as if referring to a long-lost relative who unexpectedly shows up on one's doorstep. People said that *la crisis* was responsible for every malady that afflicted them, a deus ex machina that was cause, not effect. "Because of *la crisis*, I lost my job . . ." Because of *la crisis*, you borrowed a thousand dollars and risked your life sneaking across the U.S.-Mexico border.

I spent the better part of Lent adjusting to life in Mexico City, the biggest metropolis on earth, to which I had just moved. I wasted endless hours in bureaucratic queues (phone company, water and power, immigration) that looked more like soup lines. In the evenings, I sat in my apartment writing at a desk next to soot-streaked windows that looked down upon strangely empty streets—strange for the fact that there were some twenty million souls in the immediate vicinity.

And yet Mexico City, capital of a nation in tatters, approached Easter with rapturous anticipation; holy was the great highland city whose belly button the gods tickle to remind it that no matter how poor, crowded, contaminated, or violent, it was still just an inch below heaven. If you stared into the zinc-tinted pall hanging over the valley long enough, celestial forms came into view, writhing in the smog-ether.

But the actual heavens were something else again. There had been several smog alerts since Ash Wednesday. Pigeons fell from the skies, asphyxiated. Head pounding, I wandered the labyrinth, breathing in Volkswagen fumes and smoking Mexican Marlboros, at one with one of the world's last armies of True Smokers. Mexico City dwellers love to show off their tobacco prowess despite, or precisely because of, the fact that they live in the most polluted city on earth. I spat black balls into my handkerchief.

La crisis was, above all else, a public event. Yes, there was brooding and violence inside homes, within families—in the tabloids, we were treated to the typical tales of husbands chopping up their wives and sons killing their parents. In this family-values country, you could rest assured that if you were murdered the last face you'd see would be that of a friend or relative.

But the pressure of *la crisis* was too great to bear in private. Every two weeks, *la quincena* came, the bimonthly payday, and we spilled into the streets, into cantinas and dance halls and strip joints. God knows where the money came from. But I'd seen it before, this end-of-the-world excess, in the barrios of San Salvador during the darkest days of the civil war, in Managua at the height of the U.S. embargo against the Sandinista regime, in Havana back when Castro prohibited mention of the word *glasnost* and quarantined the island from contact with the outside world. When apocalypse is at hand there's nothing left to lose, and inhibitions fall. There might not have been enough money to pay the rent, buy clothes, or even eat decently, but, by God, there was enough for a round of drinks. Solidarity.

Thus, Mexicans escaped *la crisis* through the spectacle of public ritual. No one ever did anything alone. If you had a doctor's appointment, you called up your best friend; he'd take the day off from work to escort you, and stand by your side even during the embarrassing rubber-gloved examination. Same thing for trips to the bank, to get a haircut, to buy groceries. There was always great chatter as people lined up to do their business.

The ultimate Mexican public ritual, the fiesta, derives its tremendous energy from the tension between spirit and flesh, between Indian and Iberian, between Christianity and pagan pantheism—in a word, from Mexico's "mestizo," or mixed blood and culture. *La crisis* only poured fuel on the fire. In 1995, December 12 (the Virgin of Guadalupe's feast day), 24, and 31 were days of national paroxysm. On Valentine's Day, practically every hotel in the country, from the swank joints to the barrio hovels, hung a No Vacancy sign and ecstatic shrieks echoed along the halls: a national fuck. The provinces partied as hard as the capital; every town has a patron saint and the feast days were excuses for weeklong bacchanals on the order of decadent Rome. In the Indian territories, pagan agricultural rites only thinly disguised as Catholic were celebrated as never before. What all these fiestas had in common was that we celebrated the spirit *through* the flesh. We alternated between the extremes of mortified piety and Dionysian abandon.

And then there was Easter.

Throughout Lent, Mexicans performed the Catholic rite of abstinence and fasting, physically representing the economic collapse with their very bodies. Economic forces, after all, are invisible but for the effect they have on our physical form: where we live, what we eat, what we wear, how we dance. As Lent drew to a close, Mexico prepared to nail itself to the cross.

A gray wind blows in Iztapalapa. The rains of summer are months away and the dust of ancient, infertile earth rises in choking clouds. Lying on a fallow plain south of downtown Mexico City, the district of Iztapalapa, by the looks of things, was a rough-and-tumble barrio long before the Spaniards arrived. It has the color of old poverty: dark brown, almost chocolate-brown skin, the color of little or no crossbreeding. Iztapalapa's Indian population was poor around the time of the Conquest, and it's poor now.

I come up from the bowels of the metro into a plaza adorned with graffiti murals, of the officially sanctioned variety. There are eco-sensitive messages, tributes to the dead of the great quake of 1985. And a monument to *la crisis*: ESTAMOS EN LAS MANOS DE DIOS (We Are in the Hands of God), reads a banner flowing above the two hands of the Great One, which cradle a cityscape rendered postapocalyptically with skyscrapers become tombstones and a blood glow tinting the twilight sky.

Iztapalapa is famous for two things: a soaring crime rate inspired by *la crisis* (which led authorities to temporarily deploy regular army troops on its streets) and the best *representación* of the Passion in all of Mexico. The pageantry of the event is on the order of Cecil B. DeMille—practically every barrio resident plays a part. In the United States right now, people are watching *The Ten*

Commandments and *The Greatest Story Ever Told* on television, preparing for quiet Passover or Easter family gatherings and religious services. But in Mexico, half the population, from the capital to the Indian countryside, is starring in its own version of the Passion.

It is the 153rd annual *representación* in Iztapalapa (there is a region in the state of Guerrero where the ritual goes back four hundred years), and locals speak of *la tradición* with mystical reverence. The peso may have tumbled, we can't buy ham for Easter, my son was mugged last night, but we're keeping tradition alive! Just because there's a Price Club in every major city doesn't mean that Mexico has lost its essence. If Mexico didn't stop being an Indian nation five hundred years ago—mestizo identity, after all, is at least half pre-Columbian—why should it now? Still, Iztapalapa is a place contaminated by the germ of restlessness. Indians migrate from the countryside looking for the better life in the city; often, after a generation or two of urban poverty, they hit the road again, trying their luck in the States.

The barrio is decked out for the Passion: fully costumed Roman soldiers, Samaritan women, Pharisees walk the streets, snacking and smoking, shooting the breeze. But it's the *nazarenos*, the Nazarenes, who are omnipresent, roving packs of teenage boys who've built their own crosses and had their mothers stitch together simple white robes with purple sashes so they can play Jesus as penance. Five thousand or so *nazarenos* trudge along the streets of Iztapalapa this year, straining under crosses weighing up to ninety kilos. Many of the kids have been training for months.

There are dozens of simultaneous *representaciones*. A megaspectacle plays out in the plaza on a stage about fifty yards long, floodlit by arc lamps and ringed by a bevy of Televisa remote trucks that transmit the performances live nationwide.

The *representación* of the Last Supper takes place. There are easily 100,000 people gathered in the plaza before the stage, but the concentration on the scene is absolute; the only sound that can be heard, aside from the dialogue, is the hum of the remote trucks. Judas rises from the table. He frets, wrings his hands. He paces back and forth interminably, throwing anguished looks at Jesus, at the disciples, at us. The roles are taken so seriously by the residents of Iztapalapa that the brave souls who play Judas are occasionally shunned by their neighbors, as if by representing Judas they're actually betraying Jesus himself.

The Last Supper table is carted away by stagehands; foam rocks and potted trees are rolled in for the Gethsemane scene. The Iztapalapa resident who has played Jesus for the last six years pleads, with old-school theatricality, to "let this cup pass from me" while the disciples lie sleeping a few feet away.

Then the chaos: Pharisees and scribes rush in, Judas offers his last kiss, a sword is drawn, an ear is lopped off, the disciples scatter, and finally Pilate: "Which of the two do you wish that I release to you?" And the entire plaza, every last man, woman, and child, as per *tradición*, shouts "BARABBAS!"

Afterward, the crowd begins to disperse, but thousands of people remain in the plaza overnight, laying down blankets and passing around *champurrado* and *atole*, hot beverages that predate the Conquest. These fervent Indian Catholics will stay up with the Savior on the longest night of his life, the night before his death. They will also get the best seats for his crucifixion.

Good Friday begins as a startlingly clear day; somehow, we've been given a respite from the smog. Legions of visitors—an estimated two million—descend on Iztapalapa. The army of vendors fares well among the multitudes as the wait for the Crucifixion grows longer and hotter (the Red Cross tends to hundreds of sunstroke victims), selling crucifixes, sunglasses, cardboard visors, caps, mango, papaya, and bottles of Coke, Sprite, and Fanta chilled atop slabs of ice that drip puddles into the gray dust.

I join the *nazarenos* on their serpentine path through the barrios. Five thousand Christs accompanied by the sound of the wood of five thousand crosses dragging along the asphalt. The kids range in age from preteens with crosses only about four feet long to twenty-somethings with several years of *representación* experience, carrying the better part of a tree over their shoulders. Some of the crosses are painted black, others red. Some are carved with flowery designs, others varnished so well they look like they're encased in glass.

The pilgrimage begins at seven in the morning and winds through the better part of Iztapalapa before arriving at Golgotha in the late afternoon. The *nazarenos* start out in high spirits, perhaps guilty just a tad of the sin of pride. But by noon, the Red Cross is carting kids off on stretchers. It's the feet that suffer the most. A good many Christs go barefoot—on asphalt baking in the hot sun and sprinkled with broken glass. Some wear Ace bandages, which soon grow filthy and unravel. Others wear cheap huaraches; these, too, fall apart after a few kilometers. The kids jump onto pieces of cardboard—thrown down on the sizzling street by store owners along the route—and then, wincing, back onto the asphalt.

At times, the procession grows scraggly as, overpowered by the sun, kids fall out of the ranks, but the organizers rush in, shouting and whistling like Romans. I stand in the shade of a corner general store, drinking Pepsi and smoking Marlboros along with the crowd of onlookers, and suddenly there appears before us the most unlikely of *samaritanas*, dressed in a floor-length red velvet cloak but showing an inordinate amount of cleavage, her face made up like a transvestite's. Maybe she *is* a transvestite, who knows? The sight of this sexy Samaritan, eyeliner running down her cheeks, taking uncertain steps in five-inch stilettos is too much for the gaggle of mothers and grandmothers around me. "In *heels!*" cries one of them with glee. "Now that's really a love of art!"

Amazingly, the vast majority of the procession will make it to Golgotha, to Cerro de la Muerte. A fourteen-year-old carrying a cross he claims weighs seventy kilos says: "My father did it, my older brothers did it, now it is my turn to fulfill the tradition." And an eighteen-year-old wearing a real crown of thorns, drops of dried blood on his temples: "There's no pain that I couldn't bear with my faith in the Lord." Every kid is followed by a support crew of siblings, parents, and grandparents urging them on, carrying water bottles and cotton and alcohol to swab the aching, blistered feet.

Again and again the theme of *la crisis* comes up in snippets of casual conversation. Seems that there are more *nazarenos* since the peso fell. Seems like there are fewer vendors but more *tradición*, more *devoción*. A barrio grandmother sums it up: "It's the crisis that is making people come closer to God. More sinners, more penitents. The problem is, the really big sinners, *los políticos hijos de la chingada*—politico sons of bitches—never do their penance. We wind up doing it for them."

Finally, close to three in the afternoon, the *nazarenos* and *romanos* and *samaritanas* make their tattered, triumphal approach to Cerro de la Muerte. Kids sprint the final yards up the hill, throw down their crosses, collapse, strip off robes and T-shirts. Soon the hill is littered with five thousand crosses and the panting, half-naked bodies of five thousand brown Christs. Three great crosses crown Golgotha, with five thousand *nazareno* crosses scattered helterskelter at their feet.

Surrounding the hill, held back from the *representación* area by a chain-link fence, are the two million onlookers. The sea of people in all directions is like a huge, unified organism, a great jellyfish, nudging its way ever closer to the *representación*, straining against the fence and the army of cops, Indian kids armed with ancient service revolvers.

Now trumpets blast. Romans on white stallions charge up the hill.

The proclaimer: "And having committed these and many other crimes . . . we condemn him and sentence him to be taken along the streets of the Holy City of Jerusalem, crowned with thorns and with a chain about his neck, carrying his own cross, and accompanied by two criminals, Dismas and Gestas, unto Golgotha, and that there he be crucified between the two criminals, where he will hang until dead."

He is nailed to the cross, the ninety-kilo cross that he himself built, the one that he has dragged in procession through Iztapalapa every day since Palm Sunday. The sound of the hammer resounds through the great banks of speakers. Stage blood spouts from hands and feet. A camera crane moves in close for the dizzying Scorsese shot.

Christ, Dismas, and Gestas writhe on their crosses, and all of Mexico's children see themselves. On Golgotha hangs every dream ever denied in this land: the three crucified might as well be named Benjamín, Jaime, and Salvador Chávez.

In the final moments of the Passion, the gray wind of Iztapalapa rises in great clouds above the massive crowd. It is the gray of the great dust of the city, not just the arid topsoil of the Cerro but particles of ash from the billion cigarettes of the chain-smoking city, refuse from the garbage dumps on every street corner in the barrios, sooty exhaust from the trucks and taxis and the passenger cars of the rich and poor, especially the poor with their jury-rigged eight-cylinder smoking Chevys—the dust of poverty, the dust of corruption, the dust of hell on earth.

As we bring handkerchiefs to our faces and rub our eyes, everything that was white turns gray: the robes of the *nazarenos*, the blocks of ice at the vending stalls, the pages of my notebook.

On this Good Friday the holy, fallen country has come to watch itself die.

And live.

It is accomplished.

SANDRA CISNEROS

(1954–)

Sandra Cisneros was born in Chicago, the only daughter in a family of seven children. She immortalized the Mexican neighborhoods of her youth in her two novels, *The House on Mango Street* (1991) and *Caramelo* (2002). *The House on Mango Street* has sold more than two million copies and is required reading in classrooms across the country. *Caramelo* was selected as a notable book of the year by several newspapers including *The New York Times*, the *Los Angeles Times*, and the *San Francisco Chronicle*, and was nominated for the Orange Prize in Britain. Her collection of short stories, *Woman Hollering Creek and Other Stories* (1991), was awarded the PEN Center West Award for Best Fiction of 1991 and the Lannan Foundation Literary Award. Cisneros's lyrical prose, distinct voice, and creative structuring have made her not only one of the foremost Latina writers in the United States, but one of the most celebrated writers in contemporary literature. Her collections of poetry include *Bad Boys* (1980), *My Wicked Wicked Ways* (1987), and *Loose Woman* (1994).

YOU BRING OUT THE MEXICAN IN ME

You bring out the Mexican in me.
The hunkered thick dark spiral.
The core of a heart howl.
The bitter bile.
The tequila *lágrimas* on Saturday all
through next weekend Sunday.

You are the one I'd let go the other loves for,
surrender my one-woman house.
Allow you red wine in bed,
even with my vintage lace linens.
Maybe. Maybe.

For you.

You bring out the Dolores del Río in me.
The Mexican spitfire in me.
The raw *navajas*, glint and passion in me.
The raise Cain and dance with the rooster-footed
    devil in me.
The spangled sequin in me.
The eagle and serpent in me.
The *mariachi* trumpets of the blood in me.
The Aztec love of war in me.
The fierce obsidian of the tongue in me.
The *berrinchuda*, *bien-cabrona* in me.
The Pandora's curiosity in me.
The pre-Columbian death and destruction in me.
The rainforest disaster, nuclear threat in me.
The fear of fascists in me.
Yes, you do. Yes, you do.

You bring out the colonizer in me.
The holocaust of desire in me.
The Mexico City '85 earthquake in me.
The Popocatepetl/Ixtaccíhuatl in me.
The tidal wave of recession in me.
The Agustín Lara hopeless romantic in me.
The *barbacoa taquitos* on Sunday in me.
The cover the mirrors with cloth in me.

Sweet twin. My wicked other,
I am the memory that circles your bed nights,
that tugs you taut as moon tugs ocean.
I claim you all mine,
arrogant as Manifest Destiny.
I want to rattle and rent you in two.
I want to defile you and raise hell.
I want to pull out the kitchen knives,
dull and sharp, and whisk the air with crosses.
Me sacas lo mexicana en mi,
like it or not, honey.

You bring out the Uled-Nayl in me.
The stand-back-white-bitch in me.
The switchblade in the boot in me.
The Acapulco cliff diver in me.
The *Flecha Roja* mountain disaster in me.
The *dengue* fever in me.
The *¡Alarma!* murderess in me.
I could kill in the name of you and think
it worth it. Brandish a fork and terrorize rivals,
female and male, who loiter and look at you,
languid in your light. Oh,

I am evil. I am the filth goddess Tlazoltéotl.
I am the swallower of sins.
The lust goddess without guilt.
The delicious debauchery. You bring out
the primordial exquisiteness in me.
The nasty obsession in me.
The corporal and venial sin in me.
The original transgression in me.

Red ocher. Yellow ocher. Indigo. Cochineal.
Piñón. Copal. Sweetgrass. Myrrh.
All you saints, blessed and terrible,
Virgen de Guadalupe, diosa Coatlicue,
I invoke you.

Quiero ser tuya. Only yours. Only you.
Quiero amarte. Atarte. Amarrarte.
Love the way a Mexican woman loves. Let
me show you. Love the only way I know how.

RITUAL

AND MYTH

*Día de los Muertos
and Beyond*

ERNA FERGUSSON

(1 8 4 6 – 1 9 6 4)

A native of Albuquerque, New Mexico, Erna Fergusson worked as a teacher until the outbreak of World War I. During the war she joined the American Red Cross as Home Service Secretary and Staff Supervisor for New Mexico, and, after her travels all over the state, started working as a reporter for the *Albuquerque Herald*. During this time, Fergusson formed a partnership with Ethel Hickey to operate a tour company that guided tourists to the Indian Pueblos in New Mexico and to the Navajo and Hopi reservations in New Mexico and Arizona. Alfred Knopf encouraged her to write about her experiences, and her first book, *Dancing Gods* (1931), was the result. She followed this with a number of books on the American Southwest and Latin America, including *Fiesta in Mexico* (1934), *Guatemala* (1937), and *Venezuela* (1939), *Our Southwest* (1940), *Our Hawaii* (1942), *Chile* (1943), *Cuba* (1946), *Albuquerque* (1947), and *Murder and Mystery in New Mexico* (1948).

In this excerpt from *Fiesta in Mexico*, Fergusson writes about Mexico's famous Día de los Muertos (Day of the Dead). On November 2, cemeteries all over Mexico are filled with families bringing food, flowers, and candles to the graves of their deceased loved ones. Though it later merged with the Catholic holidays of All Saints' Day and All Souls' Day, this celebration is thought to have started with the Aztecs, who originally celebrated it in August. The dancing skeletons and candy skulls are particular to Mexico. As Fergusson writes, "Mexico is probably the only country in the world where a person may look forward to his own death, his own funeral, his own grave."

At ten o'clock every house was locked and everyone was asleep, except one group of men who wandered singing alabanzas, their

white calzones and white hats separated by swinging dark sarapes
with white fringes. Sometimes they stood outside to sing, sometimes their muffled voices came from a closed house. Our host,
Ángel Guzmán, was watching his family's altar to the dead, where
a beautiful old crucifix stood among the flowers, while his wife
and daughters slept. At eleven o'clock women began to come out
of the houses carrying things. Every year Janitzio has a special
duck-hunt to provide food for *los muertos*, so many of the covered
bowls were filled with duck. They brought other food, and
flowers—all bought and paid for, for Janitzio raises not one
blossom—or square frames with a cross on top, covered thickly
with the usual calendulas. Close to, it appeared that the cross-
pieces of the frames were hung with oranges, bananas, bread,
candy shoes, skulls, coffins, and dolls. Women and children
walked softly, chatting, first a scattering few and then more and
more until they formed a silent dark procession moving along the
walled lanes which rise to the cemeteries. One is a paved square
between the church and its bell-tower, where boys were pounding
the bells, giggling and calling. The other, larger panteón runs
along under the cliff which is the island's crown, and above the
roofs of the houses in the main street. It is long and narrow, with
a colonial gateway at one end and a chapel at the other. There is
not a gravestone here as in the other panteón, but in the center
rose a tall frame like the one the women carried, with calla lilies
tied to the cross on top and calendulas massed solid on all its
braces. Women knelt to scrape away the weeds which had grown
over their chosen spots. I wondered if they really knew their
graves. Inside the chapel, as in the larger church of San Gerónimo, were coffins elongated out of all reasonable shape to accom-
modate the many offerings: white corn, yellow pumpkins, spiny
green chayotes, many kinds of fruit, and cooked foods. There
were candles, of course, and a few women had placed their flow-
ered frames in the temples.

At twelve o'clock the long narrow panteón was like a fairyland, or a Christmas tree. Hundreds of graves had been cleared and decorated, thousands of candles wavered and glowed; the ground had disappeared under scattered petals, golden arches, covered bowls, and the voluminous skirts of the women, each sitting by the grave she honored. Never do the heavily pleated Tarascan skirts show to better advantage than spread in big fan-tails behind these women squatting on their heels and seeming to lean against the enormous ruff above the waist. Most of the skirts are dark blue like the rebozo, so the figures rise like dark cones among the flowers and candles. Men do not take much part in this fiesta. They were singing always, under the roofs, sometimes in warm rich tones, sometimes with the unmistakable breaks and yips of too much pulque. A few came with burdens, spread themselves in sharp white curves and angles over the big arch, and hung from its orange supports a frosty rime of ghost-white corn. At its foot they piled other fruits and vegetables, all for the priest, like the ofrendas in the chapels. In the early morning the offerings would all be loaded into a canoe with El Señor Cura and paddled off to Pátzcuaro. The priest does not often come to Janitzio, nor stay long.

In general men were out of sight, and it was ladies' night. Most Indian women's faces are sad, with the terrible burden of a life too close to want and sorrow and pain. But in the cemetery on that night of the dead I saw few signs of grief. One girl knelt alone at the head of a grave where she had scattered a few petals and placed one bowl. She held her black veil to shelter a candle from the chill wind, and in its glow her face, above a pink blouse, was truly sad. But the prevailing expression was that of the happy complacency of a woman who has made a good party and is now enjoying it. Sitting close together, the women were laughing and talking in the low Indian tones, which seem so well-bred. It was a quiet party, but a hostess responsible for it would have felt that it was good. Not gay, but everyone was having a good time.

I sat against the schoolhouse wall facing the church, my back against the base of a cross, my feet just escaping a gravestone dated 1893. A woman approached, followed by three little girls, carrying things and importantly kicking out their grown-up pleats. The woman knelt and began to lay out her offerings: four platters wrapped in crocheted tidies, six tall candles worth fifty centavos apiece, a tall arco, and an armful of yellow flowers. As she plucked and scattered petals, she greeted me, shyly at first, to see if the stranger understood, then with more assurance. The conversation took the usual lines. From where did I come, how much did it cost, how long did it take, was I soon going home? She was busy all the time placing candles and food to her liking, and her quick brown hands moved with the deftness of women who make pottery.

She was from Tzintzuntzan, she told me, and I thought it strange that she spent the Día de los Muertos here instead of there.

"I come every year," she said. "Here I have my mother-in-law," patting the stone, "and my mother is in the other panteón. Will you come there and chat with me?"

Just then it was too interesting to leave, for a youth in white was moving about in the church carrying an urn of the kind made in Santa Fe de la Laguna, smoking with the copal incense. He stopped before every image—Santiago warlike on his horse, San Gerónimo on the altar, the Guadalupe, and a gentle little Virgin in a native embroidered petticoat. Then he came out and made reverence with the smoke in every direction. It was copal, the ancient incense; probably his gestures toward the four directions were ancient too.

At two o'clock every grave was served. The moon was high, the lake was silver and mauve, with sharp glitters where a frosty breeze turned the water. The stars were very distant and clear, and a few blurred lights marked the villages on the shore: Pátzcuaro, a colonial town which retreats into soft hills away from the Indian lake; Higuachio, where nasturtiums run all along the stone walls; Tzintzenguaro, where an occasional rocket slithered into the sky. Here and there a cock crowed. A fellow in an unbuttoned military jacket came into the cemetery, followed by a worried woman. His cap was crooked, his face flushed, his voice thick, and he was moved to make a speech.

"The dead are the happy ones," he wavered. "Keep your candles lit so they won't come back to suffer as we suffer. Sit there, I tell you, sit there with your offerings and don't let the dead come back." He offered this advice, over and over, the length of the graveyard, until at last the nervous woman got him away round the chapel at the other end.

The effect of a social affair continued. Little girls gave up and rolled into tight balls of sleep in their rebozos, but most of the women sat erect, against their heavy serge ruffs, smiling and correct, chatting and laughing. At four o'clock a pig wandered in at the colonial gate, got confused by the noise and lights, squealed and ran and was rushed with hisses and giggles, and finally made his unhappy way out behind the chapel. This was a delightful interlude for all, except maybe the pig, but he was a well-bred Indian pig and didn't upset a single candle or step in a single bowl of food. By that time many old women were letting their eyes close and their heads droop, to wake again with jerks.

At six o'clock a man came through the cemetery announcing that mass was about to begin in the church. Nobody moved. Bells rang. The boys in the campanile were still noisily awake. In the church a dozen women sat before their offerings, and fresh candles had been placed on the altars and around the lengthy coffins. In the dusty choir loft a beautiful dark Indian youth sat at an organ he had draped, certainly with no idea of its striking effect, with his brilliant red sarape. His touch on the instrument was good, his voice excellent. Only his Latin needed occasional prompting by the priest as the two of them sang the complete high mass. There was one red-robed acolyte and a man in white calzones and shirt to serve. Otherwise the padre waited on himself, changing unaided from heavy chasuble to cape, chanting in a rich and culti-vated voice. Once he moved into the apse and made slow progress around the coffins, scattering incense and holy water, stepping carefully around the kneeling women, who were always busy with the candles, picking off wax, turning the flame, blowing out one and lighting another. The church service only added to the im-pression that the Day of the Dead, at Janitzio anyway, is Indian and not Catholic. Less than thirty people were in the church, mostly women who had been there all the time, and through the chanting of the mass there ran on continuously the light laughing chatter of the women sitting on the graves outside.

LANGSTON HUGHES

(1902 – 67)

A major voice in the Harlem Renaissance, Langston Hughes forever changed American literature, making the blues and jazz central to the rhythm and language of his poetry. In his autobiography, *The Big Sea* (1940), Hughes writes about visiting his father in Mexico. His father had had legal training in the American South, but wasn't admitted to the bar there, so he went to Mexico where he was admitted to the bar and practiced law. He became a successful businessman, and bought property in Mexico City and a ranch in the country. Langston Hughes visited as a young man, later recalling that "that summer in Mexico was the worst I have ever known." Eventually Hughes started venturing from the ranch into Mexico City, and in this passage he writes about developing his skills as a writer while describing the bullfight.

BULLFIGHTS

Almost every week-end that winter, now that I was earning my own money, I went to the bullfights in Mexico City. Rudolfo Gaona was the famous Mexican matador of the day, a stocky Indian of great art and bravery. Sanchez Mejias was there from Spain that season, greatly acclaimed, as well as Juan Silveti, and a younger fighter called Juan Luis de la Rosa, who did not win much favor with the crowd. One afternoon, in the sunset, at the end of a six-bull *corrida* (bulls from the Duque de Veragua), I saw de la Rosa trying to kill his final bull amidst a shower of cushions, canes, paper bags, and anything else throwable that an irate crowd could hurl at him. But he stuck it out, and finally the enormous animal slid to his knees, bleeding on the sand. But the matador was soundly hissed as he left the ring.

At the annual festival bullfight for the charities of la Cava-donga, when the belles of Mexico City, in their lace mantillas, drove about the arena in open carriages preceding the fight, and the National Band played, and the *Presidente de la Republica* was there, and Sanchez Mejias made the hair stand on your head and cold chills run down your back with the daring and beauty of his *veronicas*, after the fight there was a great rush into the ring on the part of many of the young men in the crowd, to lift the famous fighters on their shoulders or to carry off a pair of golden bande-rillas as a souvenir, with the warm blood still on them. I dived for the ring, too, the moment the fight was over. In leaping the *barrera*, I tore my only good trousers from knee to ankle—but I got my banderillas.

After the fights, I would usually have supper with the three charming and aging Mexican sisters, the Patiños, friends of my father's, who lived near the Zócalo, just back of the cathedral, and who always invited me to vespers. To please them, I would go to vespers, and I began to love the great, dusky, candle-lighted interi-ors of the vast Mexican churches, smoky with incense and filled with sad virgins and gruesome crucifixes with real thorns on the Christ-head, and what seemed to be real blood gushing forth from His side, thick and red as the blood of the bulls I had seen killed in the afternoon. In the evenings I might go to see Margarita Xirgu, or Virginia Fabregas in some bad Spanish play, over-acted and sticky like the cakes in our Toluca sweet shop.

Meanwhile, ambitiously, I began to try to write prose. I tried to write about a bullfight, but could never capture it on paper. Bull-fights are very hard things to put down on paper—like trying to describe the ballet.

Bullfights must be seen in all their strength of vigorous and graceful movement and glitter of sun on sleek hides and silken suits spangled with gold and silver and on the sharp points of the banderillas and on the thin blades of the swords. Bullfights must be heard, the music barbaric and Moorish, the roar of the crowd, the grunt of the bull, the cry of the gored horse, the trumpet signalling to kill, the silence when a man is gored. They must be smelt, dust and tobacco and animals and leather, sweat and blood and the scent of death. Then the cry of glory when a great kill is made and the flutter of thousands of handkerchiefs, with roses thrown at the feet of the triumphant matador, as he is awarded the tail and ears of the bull. Or the hiss of scorn when the fighter has been cowardly or awkward.

Then the crowd pouring out into the sunset, and the fighters covered with sand and spattered with blood, gliding off to their hotels in swift, high-powered cars; the women on the street selling lottery tickets; beggars; and men giving out cards to houses of pleasure; and the police clearing a passage for the big Duesenbergs of the rich; and the naked bulls hanging beneath the arena, skinned, ready for the market.

A bullfight is like a very moving play—except that the fight is real, unrehearsed, and no two *corridas* are ever the same. Of course, the bull gets killed. But sometimes, the man dies first. It is not a game or a sport. It's life playing deliberately with death. Except that death is alive, too, taking an active part.

GARY JENNINGS

(1928–99)

Gary Jennings worked in advertising and as a newspaper reporter before join-
ing the U.S. Army and serving as a correspondent in the Korean War from
1958 to 1961. After the war, he decided he wanted to write full-time, so he
moved to San Miguel de Allende in Mexico.

He lived in Mexico for twelve years, and during this time he became fascinated with Aztec culture and researched it extensively. His novel *Aztec* (1980)
is a tale of lust and human sacrifice set when the Aztec Empire had reached
its zenith and the Spanish arrived. The narrator, Mixtil, or Dark Cloud, becomes
a scribe, then a warrior. Later, he becomes wealthy as a traveling merchant,
exploring every part of what the Aztecs called The One World—the far lands
of mountains, jungles, deserts, sea coasts. He dictates his story to a Spanish
"conqueror." In this excerpt, the narrator describes an Aztec festival and inter-
prets some of the complexities of their calendar. Jennings's other historical
novels based on the Aztecs include *Aztec Autumn* (1997) and the posthumously published *Aztec Blood* (2001).

Yes, Your Excellency, I know that you are most particularly interested in our former religious observances, hence your attendance
here today. Although I was never a priest, nor much of a friend to
priests, I will explain the dedication of the Great Pyramid—the
manner of it and the significance of it—as well as I can.

If that was not the most resplendent, populous, and awesome
celebration ever held in the history of the Mexíca, it certainly outdid all others I beheld in my time. The Heart of the One World
was a solid mass of people, of colorful fabrics, of perfumes, of

feather plumes, of flesh; of gold, of body heat, of jewels, of sweat. One reason for the crowding was that lanes had to be kept open—by cordons of guards, their arms linked, struggling to contain the jostling mob—so the lines of prisoners could march to the pyramid and ascend to the sacrificial altar. But the spectator crush was also due to the fact that the standing-room in the plaza had been reduced by the building of numerous new temples over the years, not to mention the gradually spreading bulk of the Great Pyramid itself.

Since Your Excellency never saw it, perhaps I had better describe that icpac tlamanacáli. Its base was square, one hundred and fifty paces from one corner to the next, the four sides sloping inward as they rose, until the pyramid's flat summit measured seventy paces to a side. The staircase ascending its front or western incline was actually two stairways, one each for those persons climbing and descending, separated by an ornamental gutter for blood to flow down. Fifty and two stairs of steep risers and narrow treads led to a terrace that encircled the pyramid a third of the way up. Then another flight of one hundred and four steps culminated in the platform on top, with its temples and their appurtenances. At either side of every thirteenth step of the staircase stood the stone image of some god, major or minor, its stone fists holding aloft a tall pole from which floated a white feather banner.

To a man standing at the very bottom of the Great Pyramid, the structures on top were invisible. From the bottom he could see only the broad dual staircase ascending, appearing to narrow, and seeming to lead even higher than it did—into the blue sky or, on other occasions, into the sunrise. A xochimíqui trudging up the stairs toward his Flowery Death must have felt that he was truly climbing toward the very heavens of the high gods.

But when he reached the top, he would find first the small pyramidal sacrificial stone and behind that the two temples. In a

sense, those teocáltin represented war and peace, for the one on
the right was the abode of Huitzilopóchtli, responsible for our
military prowess, and in the one on the left dwelt Tlaloc, responsible for our harvests and peacetime prosperity. Perhaps there
should rightly have been a third teocáli for the sun, Tonatíu, but
he already had a separate sanctuary on a more modest pyramid
elsewhere in the plaza, as did several other important gods. There
was also in the plaza the temple in which were ranked the images
of numerous gods of subordinate nations.

The new temples of Tlaloc and Huitzilopóchtli, atop the new
Great Pyramid, were but square stone rooms, each containing a
hollow stone statue of the god, his mouth wide open to receive
nourishment. But each temple was made much taller and more
impressive by a towering stone façade or roof comb: Huitzilopóchtli's indented with angular and red-painted designs, Tlaloc's
indented with rounded and blue-painted designs. The body of the
pyramid was predominately a gleaming almost-silver gesso white,
but the two serpentine banisters, one along each flank of the dual
staircase, were painted with reptilian scales of red, blue, and green,
and their big snake heads, stretching out at the ground level, were
entirely covered with beaten gold.

When the ceremony began, at the first full light of day, the chief
priests of Tlaloc and Huitzilopóchtli, with all their assistants, were
fussing around the temples at the top of the pyramid, doing
whatever it is that priests do at the last moment. On the terrace
encircling the pyramid stood the more distinguished guests:
Tenochtítlan's Revered Speaker Ahuítzotl, naturally, with Tex-
cóco's Revered Speaker Nezahualpíli and Tlácopan's Revered
Speaker Chimalpopóca. There were also the rulers of other cities,
provinces, and nations—from far-flung Mexíca domains, from the
Tzapotéca lands, from the Mixtéca, from the Totonáca, from the
Huaxtéca, from the nations whose names I did not then even

know. Not present, of course, was that implacably inimical ruler, old Xicoténca of Texcála, but Yquíngare of Michihuácan was there.

Think of it, Your Excellency. If your Captain-General Cortés had arrived in the plaza on that day, he could have accomplished our overthrow with one swift and easy slaughter of almost all our rightful rulers. He could have proclaimed himself, there and then, the lord of practically all of what is now New Spain, and our lead-erless peoples would have been hard put to dispute him. They would have been like a beheaded animal which can twitch and flail only futilely. We would have been spared, I now realize, much of the misery and suffering we later endured. But *yyo ayyo!* On that day we celebrated the might of the Mexíca, and we did not even suspect the existence of such things as white men, and we sup-posed that our roads and our days led ahead into a limitless future. Indeed, we did have some years of vigor and glory still before us, so I am glad—even knowing what I know—I am glad that no alien intruder spoiled that splendid day.

The morning was devoted to entertainments. There was much singing and dancing by the troupes from this very House of Song in which we now sit, Your Excellency, and they were far more pro-fessionally skilled than any performers I had seen or heard in Tex-cóco or Xaltócan—though to me none equaled the grace of my lost Tzitzitlíni. There were the familiar instruments: the single thunder drum, the several god drums, the water drums, the sus-pended gourds, the reed flutes and shinbone flutes and sweet-potato flutes. But the singers and dancers were also accompanied by other instruments of a complexity I had not seen elsewhere. One was called "the warbling waters," a flute which sent its notes bubbling through a water jug, with an echo effect. There was another flute, made of clay, shaped rather like a thick dish, and its player did not move his lips or fingers; he moved his head about while he blew into the mouthpiece, so that a small clay ball inside the flute rolled to stop one hole or another around its rim. And, of course, of every kind of instrument there were many. Their combined music must have been audible to any stay-at-homes in every community around all the five lakes.

The musicians, singers, and dancers performed on the lower steps of the pyramid and on a cleared space directly in front of it. Whenever they tired and required a rest, their place was taken by athletic performers. Strong men lifted prodigious weights of stone, or tossed nearly naked beautiful girls back and forth to each other as if the girls had been feathers. Acrobats outdid grasshoppers and rabbits with their leaping, tumbling antics. Or they stood upon each other's shoulders—ten, then twenty, then forty men at a time—to form human representations of the Great Pyramid itself. Comic dwarfs performed grotesque and indecent pantomimes. Jugglers kept incredible numbers of tlachtli balls spinning aloft, from hand to hand, in intricate looping patterns. . . .

No, Your Excellency, I do not mean to imply that the morning's entertainments were a mere diversion (as you put it) to lighten the horror to come (as you put it), and I do not know what you mean when you mutter of "bread and circuses." Your Excellency must not infer that those merriments were in any wise irreverent. Every performer dedicated his particular trick or talent to the gods we honored that day. If the performances were not somber but frolicsome, it was to cajole the gods into a mood to receive with gratitude our later offerings.

Everything done that morning had some connection with our religious beliefs or customs or traditions, though the relation might not be immediately evident to a foreign observer like Your Excellency. For example, there were the tocotíne, come on invitation from the Totonáca oceanside lands where their distinctive sport had been invented—or perhaps god-inspired. Their performance required the erection of an exceptionally tall tree trunk in a socket specially drilled in the plaza marble. A live bird was placed in that hole, and mashed by the insertion of the tree trunk, so that its blood would lend the tocotíne the strength they would need for flying. Yes, flying.

The erected pole stood almost as tall as the Great Pyramid. At its top was a tiny wooden platform, no bigger than a man's circled arms. Twined all down the pole was a loose meshing of stout ropes. Five Totonáca men climbed the pole to its top, one carrying a flute and a small drum tied to his loincloth, the other four unencumbered except for a profusion of bright feathers. In fact, they were totally naked except for those feathers glued to their arms. Arriving at the platform, the four feathered men somehow sat around the edge of the wooden piece, while the fifth man slowly, precariously got to his feet and stood upon it.

There on that constricted space he stood, dizzyingly high, and then he stamped one foot and then the other, and then he began to dance, accompanying himself with flute and drum. The drum he patted and pounded with one hand while his other manipulated the holes of the flute on which he blew. Though everyone watching from the plaza below was breathlessly quiet, the music came down to us as only the thinnest tweedling and thumping. Meanwhile, the other four tocotíne were cautiously knotting the pole's rope ends around their ankles, but we could not see it, so high up they were. When they were ready, the dancing man made some signal to the musicians in the plaza.

Ba-ra-ROOM! There was a thunderous concussion of music and drumming that made every spectator jump, and, at the same instant, the four men atop the pole also jumped—into empty air. They flung themselves outward and spread their arms, the full length of which were feathered. Each of the men was feathered like a different bird: a red macaw, a blue fisher bird, a green parrot, a yellow toucan—and his arms were his outstretched wings. That first leap carried the tocotíne a distance outward from the platform, but then the ropes around their ankles jerked them up short. They would all have fallen back against the pole, except for the ingenious way the ropes were twined. The men's initial leap outward became a slow circling around the pole, each of the men equidistant from the others, and each still in the graceful posture of a spread-winged, hovering bird.

While the man on top went on dancing and the musicians below played a trilling, lilting, pulsing accompaniment, the four bird-men continued to circle and, as the ropes gradually unwound from the pole, they circled farther out and slowly came lower. But the men, like birds, could tilt their feathered arms so that they rose and dipped and soared up and down past each other as if they too danced—but in all the dimensions of the sky.

Each man's rope was wrapped thirteen times around and down the extent of the pole. On his final circuit, when his body was swinging in its widest and swiftest circle, almost touching the plaza pavement, he arched his body and backed his wings against the air—exactly in the manner of a bird alighting—so that he skimmed to the ground feet first, and the rope came loose, and he ran to a stop. All four did that at the same moment. Then one of them held his rope taut for the fifth man to slide down to the plaza.

If Your Excellency has read some of my previous explanations of our beliefs, you will have realized that the sport of the tocotíne was not simply an acrobatic feat, but that each aspect of it had some significance. The four fliers were partly feathered, partly flesh, like Quetzalcóatl, the Feathered Serpent. The four circling men with the dancing man among them represented our five points of the compass: north, east, west, south, and center. The thirteen turns of each rope corresponded to the thirteen day and year numbers of our ritual calendar. And four times thirteen makes fifty and two, the number of years in a sheaf of years. There were more subtle relevances—the word tocotíne means "the sowers"—but I will not expatiate on those things, for I perceive that Your Excellency is more eager to hear of the sacrificial part of the dedication ceremony.

SALMAN RUSHDIE

(1 9 4 7 –)

Salman Rushdie was born in Bombay (now Mumbai), India, educated in England, and has lived in New York City. His novels jump among many identities and places, drawing references from both pop culture and ancient religions. In 1981, he won the Booker Prize for his novel *Midnight's Children*. He's best known for his novel *The Satanic Verses* (1989), which provoked Iran's Ayatollah Khomeini to issue a *fatwa*, or death sentence, against Rushdie. He went underground, but continued to write, and in 1998 the fatwa was lifted.

In *The Ground Beneath Her Feet* (1999), Rushdie recasts the tale of Orpheus and Eurydice in an alternate reality that resembles our modern world. Mexico is the perfect setting for his collision of ancient Greek myths and rock stars from India. The story opens in the state of Guadalajara, in the famous town of Tequila. In this passage, two things Mexico is well known for—earthquakes and tequila—are brought together, just before the world-famous singer Vina, a modern Eurydice, is swallowed whole.

The afternoon heat was dry and fierce, which she loved. Before we landed, the pilot had been informed of mild earth tremors in the region, but they had passed, he reassured us, there was no reason to abort the landing. Then he cursed the French. "After each one of those tests you can count five days, one, two, three, four, five, and the ground shakes." He set the helicopter down in a dusty football field in the centre of the little town of Tequila. What must have been the town's entire police force was keeping the local population at bay. As Vina Apsara majestically descended (always a princess, she was growing into queenliness) a cry went up, just her name, *Veeenaaa*, the vowels elongated by pure longing, and I recognized, not for the first time, that in spite of all the hyperbolic revelry and public display of her life, in spite of all her star antics, her *nakhras*, she was never resented, something in her manner disarmed people, and what bubbled out of them instead of bile was a miraculous, unconditional affection, as if she were the whole earth's very own newborn child.

Call it love.

Small boys burst through the cordon, chased by perspiring cops, and then there was Don Ángel Cruz with his two silver Bentleys that exactly matched the colour of his hair, apologizing for not greeting us with an aria, but the dust, the unfortunate dust, it is always a difficulty but now with the tremor the air is full of it, please, señora, señor, and with a small cough against the back of his wrist he shepherded us into the lead Bentley, we will go at once, please, and commence the programme. He seated himself in the second vehicle, mopping himself with giant kerchiefs, the huge smile on his face held there by a great effort of will. You could almost see the heaving distraction beneath that surface of a perfect host. "That's a worried man," I said to Vina as our car drove towards the plantation. She shrugged. She had crossed the Oakland Bay Bridge going west in October 1984, test-driving a luxury car for a promotional feature in *Vanity Fair*, and on the far side she drove into a gas station, climbed out of the car and saw it lift off the ground, all four wheels, and hang there in the air like something from the future, or *Back to the Future*, anyway. At that moment the Bay Bridge was collapsing like a children's toy. There-fore, "Don't you earthquake me," she said to me in her tough-broad, disaster-vet voice as we arrived at the plantation, where Don Ángel's employees waited with straw cowboy hats to shield us from the sun and machete maestros prepared to demonstrate how one hacked an agave plant down into a big blue "pineapple" ready for the pulping machine. "Don't try and Richter me, Rai, honey. I been scaled before."

The animals were misbehaving. Brindled mongrels ran in circles, yelping, and there was a whinnying of horses. Oracular birds wheeled noisily overhead. Subcutaneous seismic activity increased, too, beneath the increasingly distended affability of Don Ángel Cruz as he dragged us round the distillery, these are our traditional wooden vats, and here are our shining new technological marvels, our capital investment for the future, our enormous investment, our investment beyond price. Fear had begun to ooze from him in globules of rancid sweat. Absently he dabbed his sodden hankies at the odorous flow, and in the bottling plant his eyes widened further with misery as he gazed upon the fragility of his fortune, liquid cradled in glass, and the fear of an earthquake began to seep damply from the corners of his eyes.

"Sales of French wines and liquors have been down since the testing began, maybe as much as twenty percent," he muttered, shaking his head. "The wineries of Chile and our own people here in Tequila have both been beneficiaries. Export demand has shot up to such a degree you would not credit it." He wiped his eyes with the back of an unsteady hand. "Why should God give us such a gift only to take it away again? Why must He test our faith?" He peered at us, as if we might genuinely be able to offer him an answer. When he understood that no answer was available, he clutched suddenly at Vina Apsara's hands, he became a supplicant at her court, driven to this act of excessive familiarity by the force of his great need. She made no attempt to free herself from his grasp.

"I have not been a bad man," Don Ángel said to Vina, in imploring tones, as if he were praying to her. "I have been fair to my employees and amiable to my children and even faithful to my wife, excepting only, let me be honest, a couple of small incidents, and these were maybe twenty years ago, señora, you are a sophisticated lady, you can understand the weaknesses of middle age. Why then should such a day come to me?" He actually bowed his head before her, relinquishing her hands now to lock his own together and rest them fearfully against his teeth.

She was used to giving absolution. Placing her freed hands on his shoulders, she began to speak to him in That Voice, she began to murmur to him as if they were lovers, dismissing the feared earthquake like a naughty child, sending it to stand in the corner, forbidding it to create any trouble for the excellent Don Ángel, and such was the miracle of her vocal powers, of the sound of her voice more than anything it might have been saying, that the distressed fellow actually stopped sweating and, with a hesitant, tentative rebirth of good cheer, raised his cherubic head and smiled. "Good," said Vina Apsara. "Now let's have lunch."

At the family firm's old hacienda, which was nowadays used only for great feasts such as this, we found a long table set in the cloisters overlooking a fountained courtyard, and as Vina entered, a mariachi band began to play. Then the motorcade arrived, and out tumbled the whole appalling menagerie of the rock world, squealing and flurrying, knocking back their host's vintage tequila as if it were beer from a party can, or wine-in-a-box, and boasting about their ride through the earth tremors, the personal assistant hissing hatred at the unstable earth as if he were planning to sue it, the manager laughing with the glee he usually displayed only when he signed up a new act on disgracefully exploitative terms, the peacock flouncing and exclamatory, the gorillas grunting monosyllabically, the Argentine guitarists at each other's throats as usual, and the drummers—ach, drummers!—shutting out the memory of their panic by launching into a tequila-lubricated series of high-volume criticisms of the mariachi band, whose leader, resplendent in a black-and-silver outfit, hurled his sombrero to the floor and was on the point of reaching for the silver six-gun strapped to his thigh, when Don Ángel intervened and, to promote a convivial spirit, offered benevolently, "Please. If you permit it, I will intent, for your diversion, to sing."

A genuine countertenor voice silences all arguments, its sidereal sweetness shaming our pettiness, like the music of the spheres. Don Ángel Cruz gave us Gluck, "*Trionfi Amore*," and the mariachi singers did a creditable job as Chorus to his Orfeo.

> *Trionfi Amore!*
> *E il mondo intiero*
> *Serva all'impero*
> *Della beltà.*

The unhappy conclusion of the Orpheus story, Eurydice lost forever because of Orpheus's backwards look, was always a problem for composers and their librettists.—Hey, Calzabigi, what's this ending you're giving me here? Such a downer, I should send folks home with their faces long like a wurst? *Hello?* Happy it up, ja!— Sure, Herr Gluck, don't get so agitato. No problem! Love, it is stronger than Hades. Love, it make the gods merciful. How's about they send her back anyway? "Get outa here, kid, the guy's crazy for you! What's one little peek?" Then the lovers throw a party, and what a party! Dancing, wine, the whole nine yards. So you got your big finish, everybody goes out humming.—Works for me. Nice going, Raniero.—Sure thing, Willibald. Forget about it.

And here it was, that showstopper finale. Love's triumph over death. *The whole world obeys the rule of beauty.* To everyone's astonishment, mine included, Vina Apsara the rock star rose to her feet and sang both soprano parts, Amor as well as Eurydice, and though I'm no expert, she sounded word and note perfect, her voice in an ecstasy of fulfillment, finally, it seemed to be saying, you've worked out what I'm for.

> *. . . E quel sospetto*
> *Che il cor tormenta*
> *Al fin diventa*
> *Felicità.*

The tormented heart doesn't just find happiness: it *becomes happiness*. That's the story, I thought. But I misunderstood the words.

◥

The earth began to shake just as she finished, applauding her performance. The great still life of the banquet, the plates of meats and bowls of fruits and bottles of the best Cruz tequila, and even the banquet table itself, now commenced to jump and dance in Disney fashion, inanimate objects animated by the little sorcerer's apprentice, that overweening mouse; or as if moved by the sheer power of her song to join in the closing *chaconne*. As I try to remember the exact sequence of events, I find that my memory has become a silent movie. There must have been noise. Pandemonium, city of devils and their torments, could scarcely have been noisier than that Mexican town, as cracks scurried like lizards along the walls of its buildings, prying apart the walls of Don Ángel's hacienda with their long creepy fingers, until it simply fell away like an illusion, a movie façade, and through the surging dust cloud of its collapse we were returned to the pitching, bucking streets, running for our lives, not knowing which way to run but running, anyway, while tiles fell from roofs and trees were flung into the air and sewage burst upwards from the streets and houses exploded and suitcases long stored in attics began to rain down from the sky.

But I remember only silence, the silence of great horror. The silence, to be more exact, of photography, because that was my profession, so naturally it was what I turned to the moment the earthquake began. All my thoughts were of the little squares of film passing through my old cameras, Voigtländer Leica Pentax, of the forms and colours being registered therein by the accidents of movement and event, and of course by the skill or lack of it with which I managed to point the lens in the right or wrong direction at the wrong or right time. Here was the eternal silence of faces and bodies and animals and even nature itself, caught—yes—by my camera, but caught also in the grip of the fear of the unforeseeable and the anguish of loss, in the clutches of this hated metamorphosis, the appalling silence of a way of life at the moment of its annihilation, its transformation into a golden past that could never wholly be rebuilt, because once you have been in an earthquake you know, even if you survive without a scratch, that like a stroke in the heart, it remains in the earth's breast, horribly potential, always promising to return, to hit you again, with an even more devastating force.

Luis J. Rodriguez: "The Old Woman of Merida" from *Trochemoche* by Luis J. Rodriguez,
Curbstone Press, 1988. Reprinted by permission of Curbstone Press,
distributed by Consortium.

Richard Rodriguez: Excerpt from "India" from *Days of Obligation* by Richard Rodriguez,
copyright © 1992 by Richard Rodriguez. Reprinted by permission of Viking Penguin,
a division of Penguin Group (USA) Inc.

Muriel Rukeyser: "Evening Plaza, San Miguel" from *Beast in View* by Muriel Rukeyser,
copyright © 1944 by Muriel Rukeyser. Reprinted by permission of
International Creative Management, Inc.

Salman Rushdie: Excerpt from *The Ground Beneath Her Feet* by Salman Rushdie, copyright
© 1999 by Salman Rushdie. Reprinted by permission of Henry Holt & Company, LLC.

John Steinbeck: Excerpt from *The Pearl* by John Steinbeck, copyright © 1945 by
John Steinbeck, copyright renewed 1973 by Elaine Steinbeck, Thom Steinbeck,
and John Steinbeck IV. Reprinted by permission of Viking Penguin,
a division of Penguin Group (USA) Inc.

Edward Weston: Excerpt from *The Daybooks of Edward Weston*, text by Edward Weston,
copyright © 1961, 1973 by Arizona Board of Regents, Center for Creative
Photography (originally published by George Eastman House, 1961; subsequently
published by Aperature, 1990). Reprinted by permission of the Center for Creative
Photography, The University of Arizona, Tucson.

Tennessee Williams: Excerpt from *The Night of the Iguana* by Tennessee Williams, from
The Theatre of Tennessee Williams, Vol. IV, copyright © 1972 by The University of the
South. Reprinted by permission of New Directions Publishing Corp.